Leading Systemic School Improvement Series

...helping change leaders transform entire school systems

This Rowman & Littlefield Education series provides change leaders in school districts with a collection of books written by prominent authors with an interest in creating and sustaining whole-district school improvement. It features young, relatively unpublished authors with brilliant ideas, as well as authors who are cross-disciplinary thinkers.

Whether an author is prominent or relatively unpublished, the key criterion for a book's inclusion in this series is that it must address an aspect of creating and sustaining systemic school improvement. For example, books from members of the business world, developmental psychology, and organizational development are good candidates as long as they focus on creating and sustaining whole-system change in school district settings; books about building-level curriculum reform, instructional methodologies, and team communication, although interesting and helpful, are not appropriate for the series unless they discuss how these ideas can be used to create whole-district improvement.

Since the series is for practitioners, highly theoretical or research-reporting books aren't included. Instead, the series provides an artful blend of theory and practice—in other words, books based on theory and research but written in plain, easy-to-read language. Ideally, theory and research are artfully woven into practical descriptions of how to create and sustain systemic school improvement. The series is subdivided into three categories:

Why Systemic School Improvement Is Needed and Why It's Important. This is the *why*. Possible topics within this category include the history of systemic school improvement; the underlying philosophy of systemic school improvement; how systemic school improvement is different from school-based improvement; and the driving forces of standards, assessments, and accountability and why systemic improvement can respond effectively to these forces.

The Desirable Outcomes of Systemic School Improvement. This is the *what*. Possible topics within this category include comprehensive school reform models scaled up to create whole-district improvement; strategic alignment; creating a high-performance school system; redesigning a school system as a learning organization; unlearning and learning mental models; and creating an organization design flexible and agile enough to respond quickly to unanticipated events in the outside world.

How to Create and Sustain Systemic School Improvement. This is the *how*. Possible topics within this category include methods for redesigning entire school systems; tools for navigating complex change; ideas from the "new sciences" for creating systemic change; leadership methods for creating systemic change; evaluating the process and outcomes of systemic school improvement; and financing systemic school improvement.

The series editor, Dr. Francis M. Duffy, can be reached at 301-854-9800 or fmduffy@earthlink.net.

Leading Systemic School Improvement Series
Edited by Francis M. Duffy

Leading from the Eye of the Storm

Spirituality and Public School Improvement

Scott Thompson

Foreword by Margaret J. Wheatley

Rowman & Littlefield Education
Lanham, Maryland • Toronto • Oxford
2005

Published in the United States of America
by Rowman & Littlefield Education
A Division of Rowman & Littlefield Publishers, Inc.
An imprint of The Rowman & Littlefield Publishing Group, Inc.
4501 Forbes Boulevard, Suite 200, Lanham, Maryland 20706
www.rowmaneducation.com

PO Box 317
Oxford
OX2 9RU, UK

Copyright © 2005 by Scott Thompson

British Library Cataloguing in Publication Information Available

Library of Congress Cataloging-in-Publication Data

Thompson, Scott, 1958-
  Leading from the eye of the storm : spirituality and public school improvement / Scott Thompson.
    p. cm. — (Leading systemic school improvement series ; 5)
  Includes bibliographical references and index.
  ISBN 1-57886-211-6 (pbk. : alk. paper)
  1. School improvement programs. 2. Educational leadership. 3. Spiritual life. I. Title. II. Series: Leading systemic school improvement ; no. 5.

LB2822.8.T47 2005
371.2—dc22

2004026596

This book is dedicated to my parents,

Charles B. Thompson and Helen Truesdale Thompson

Contents

Foreword: The Human Spirit and School Leadership

I often work these days in cultures that have very little materially, but seem unquestionably rich in other ways. For example, in many African societies, people face unending problems and tragedies, but, even so, people still treasure their parents, laugh easily, and love being together. Some schools I've visited there have no material resources, no books or tables or blackboards, but they do have eager students and dedicated teachers. From these experiences, I've become aware of the deep impoverishment experienced by those of us who live and work in Western cultures. We have lives of material abundance, plentiful resources, and blessed ease, yet we are impoverished. And it's only getting worse.

Mother Theresa said that the greatest poverty she ever witnessed was in the United States, where people were poor in spirit. For many years, I couldn't really understand what she was saying, but now I do. For too long, we've been substituting things for people. We seem to have forgotten that real happiness is only found in meaningful lives, and in relationships where we can be generous and loving.

Nothing will end our impoverishment, nothing more will become possible, until we realize that the solutions we need can be found only in a forgotten place—the magnificent and enduring human spirit. It is only the human spirit that can deal with disturbing, even hopeless situations. It is only the human spirit that can find solid ground to stand on in the midst of chaos. It is only the human spirit that reaches out in love and forgiveness to others. It is only the human spirit that thrives in community and that withers from working alone. Archbishop Desmond Tutu expressed this beautifully: "We can be human only together."

LEADERSHIP TODAY IS SPIRITUAL

Leaders today are faced with enormous challenges, most of them not of their own doing, and for which they were not prepared by their professional training. Leaders weren't taught to deal with questions of meaning, trust, strong emotions, or uncertainty. Yet these are the prevalent issues today for all leaders.

As times grow more chaotic, as people question the meaning (and meaninglessness) of their lives, people clamor for their leaders to save and rescue them. Historically, people too often give away freedom and choose dictatorship when confronted with uncertainty. People press their leaders to stop the chaos, to make things better, to create stability. And even leaders who would never want to become controlling, those devoted to servant-leadership, walk into this trap. They want to help, so they try single-handedly to take control of the disorder. They try to create safety, to insulate people from the realities of change. They try and give answers to dilemmas that have no answers.

Or constituents, such as parents or state and federal governments, insist that their educational leaders restore control to the educational process. They pressure educators to comply with standards, to use fear and coercion as major motivators. In spite of the complexity of forces confounding public education, they press for simplistic solutions that only result in unending unintended consequences—and high levels of burnout.

In this environment, no educational leader can hope to succeed by using old style, mechanistic management. No leader can create sufficient stability for people to feel secure and safe. No leader can control the chaos, nor command people through the turbulence. Attempts to lead through command and control, through fear and coercion, are doomed to fail. Instead, leaders must support people to develop an adult relationship with uncertainty and chaos. Leaders must act on the knowledge that people would rather make a meaningful contribution than be safe. They must seek out those processes that reconnect people and that restore our faith in one another. Above all, leaders must remember that the greatest organizational resource, hidden within reach, is the human spirit.

I believe that the major work of leaders in this unsettling, uncertain time is spiritual. I say this because leaders must learn how to evoke and revitalize the human spirit present in every single person and child. This evocation cannot be done through managing by the numbers, or invoking standards, or by being the sole keeper of the school's vision. It is not accomplished through heroic leadership. It is only accomplished when *leaders act as hosts*, when they invite people into the meaningful, puzzling, scary work of the organization. Such host leaders know they cannot succeed alone, but that together, people always manage to find solutions. They remember that, no matter how difficult the challenge, people can still find joy in working together.

EVOKING HUMAN GOODNESS

All of us, not only our leaders, have a great need to remember the fact of human goodness. Human goodness seems like an outrageous "fact." Every day we are confronted with mounting evidence of the great harm we so easily do to one another. We are bombarded with global images of genocide, dislocations caused by ethnic hatred, and stories of individual violence committed daily in communities around the world. The word *evil* comes easily to our lips to explain these terrible behaviors.

And in our day-to-day lives, we are directly confronted by people who are angry, deceitful, and interested only in their own needs. In schools and communities, we struggle to find ways to work together amidst so much anger, distrust, and pettiness.

But I know that the only path to creating more harmonious and effective schools and communities is to turn to one another and depend on one another. We cannot cope, much less create, in this increasingly fast and turbulent world, without each other. We must search for human goodness.

There is no substitute for human creativity, human caring, human will. We can be incredibly resourceful, imaginative, and openhearted. We can do the impossible, learn and change quickly, and extend instant compassion to those suffering from natural and political disasters.

And these are not behaviors we use only occasionally. If you look at your daily life, how often do you figure out an answer to a problem, or find a slightly better way of doing something, or extend yourself to someone in need? Very few people go through their days as robots, doing only repetitive tasks, never noticing that anybody else is nearby. Take a moment to look around at your colleagues, students, and neighbors, and you'll see the same behaviors—people trying to be useful, trying to make some small contribution, trying to help someone else.

We have forgotten what we're capable of and let our worst natures rise to the surface. I believe we got into this sorry state partly because, for too long, we've been treating people as machines. We've tried to force people into tiny boxes, called roles and job descriptions. We've told people what to do and how they should behave.

After so many years of being bossed around, most people are exhausted, cynical, and focused on self-protection. Who wouldn't be? But it's important to remember that these negative and demoralized people (who may include us) were created by organizing processes that discount and deny our human spirits.

In too many schools, faculty, staff, and students are still being kept in boxes. They are not invited to contribute, to create, or to care about each other. Instead, it's assumed that people must be policed into good behavior. Endless policies and laws attempt to make us behave properly. Yet very few people tolerate this disrespect and constraint on their personal freedom. We become rebellious, hostile, cynical—or we shut down and look as if we died on the job. Whole districts can become deadened by coercion, but underneath the apathy and withdrawal still live human spirits that can be reawakened.

It is time to become passionate about what's best in us humans and to create schools that welcome in our creativity, contribution, and compassion. We do this by using processes that bring us together to talk to one another, listen to one another's stories, reflect together on what we're learning as we do our work. We do this by developing relationships of trust, where we do what we say, where we speak truthfully, where we refuse to act from petty self-interest. These processes and relationships have already been developed by many courageous schools, leaders, and facilitators. This book is filled with inspiring stories of some of them. I hope they inspire you to take action in your own sphere of influence.

In my experience, most educators are eager for these new processes and relationships. We know we need to work together, because daily we are overwhelmed by problems that we can't solve individually. We want to serve children. We want to contribute to society. We want to feel hopeful again.

As leaders, as educators, it is time to turn to one another, to engage in the intentional search for human goodness. In our meetings and deliberations, we can reach out and invite in those we have excluded. We can recognize that no one person or leader has the answer, that we need everybody's creativity to find our way through this strange new world. We can act from the certainty that most people do care about others, and invite them to step forward with their compassion. We can realize that "you can't hate someone whose story you know."

We wonderful human beings *are* our only hope for creating a future where the human spirit is the blessing and not the problem. We can't go it alone, we can't get there without each other, and we can't create it without relying on our fundamental human goodness.

Margaret J. Wheatley, Ed.D.
President of the Berkana Institute
and former professor of management
(www.margaretwheatley.com)

Preface: Genesis of This Book

On June 1, 2000, I boarded a jet at O'Hare International Airport in Chicago, feeling very ready to fly home after being holed up in a hotel for an intense two-day meeting. When I pulled a book of poems by William Stafford from my briefcase and read one of them, I made a discovery. Although the meeting had been intellectually stimulating and professionally satisfying (my colleagues and I had been engaged in designing an event for the development of educational leadership), it had been—speaking only for myself—an essentially spiritless experience. My soul had burrowed into a deep, unknowable place. This was the poem I opened to and read:

Ask Me

Some time when the river is ice ask me
mistakes I have made. Ask me whether
what I have done is my life. Others
have come in their slow way into
my thought, and some have tried to help
or to hurt: ask me what difference
their strongest love or hate has made.

I will listen to what you say.
You and I can turn and look
at the silent river and wait. We know
the current is there, hidden; and there
are comings and goings from miles away
that hold the stillness exactly before us.
What the river says, that is what I say.
(Stafford 1993, 126)

In the few moments it took to read this poem, I reconnected with my soul. That experience stood in such powerful contrast to the spiritually arid feeling I brought onto the plane that I was suddenly alive with a range of feelings. While what the poem aroused in me is finally ineffable, I will nevertheless try to convey some hint of the experience. It involved a heightened consciousness of inner dimension, a feeling of profundity and awe, a reawakening of what Johannes Brahms once called "the soul-power within."

"Ask Me" is among my favorite poems, and so I had read it a number of times before that moment on the plane, and I have read it many times since. While it is always satisfying and often stirring, the impact was never so profound as it was that evening, for reasons I cannot explain.

I've always loved what the poem conveys about the extent of what is hidden beneath the surface of a persona, but in that spiritual moment on the plane, I wasn't simply appreciating the way the poet's choice of words and images communicate a message. I was taken under the surface of my own experience into a deeper dimension of being. In that freshly illuminated consciousness, I found myself responding to Stafford with these words.

What I'd Want to Say to William Stafford about "Ask Me"

I read it one time
on a plane and felt
salt water drizzling
along facial contours
and losing itself
in thickets of beard.
I was not sad.
Kneeling without reaching,
I was touching
a sunlit cave
under each word.
Each sliver of light
slipped by
the vigilant deflectors,

reaching some moist
dark soulsoil.

Ask me how
real that felt
and how much I ached
to thank you.[1]

I have these kinds of experiences on planes. I think it has to do with being in a space and time that is set apart from the demands and agendas of the quotidian—a place where thoughts and feelings are freed for reflection and exploration.

A few months later, I was flying home from the leadership development event that we had been designing in that hotel in Chicago when I found myself recording these thoughts in my journal: "There is this other life in me—down there like a lake trout, usually in shadow. It is the life of soul and poetry and spiritual discovery. It is so important, and yet how often do I allow it to remain wholly submerged and unreachable. It's not difficult to see why. But at what cost?"

About a year later I discovered Parker Palmer (I had heard the name, but hadn't read his work). I first read a talk he gave entitled "The Grace of Great Things: Recovering the Sacred in Knowing, Teaching, and Learning," which includes the following observation:

I believe that movements start when individuals who feel very isolated and very alone in the midst of an alien culture, come in touch with something life-giving in the midst of a death-dealing situation. They make one of the most basic decisions a human being can make, which I have come to call the decision to live "divided no more," the decision to no longer act differently on the outside than one knows one's truth to be on the inside.[2]

The passage resonated in me deeply, because it spoke lucidly to my own spiritual struggle that had been going on for more than a decade.

I began my career, fresh out of grad school, as a high school English teacher. After two years as a full-time teacher, I went to work at the international headquarters of the church I had joined as a teenager. During this time I married a woman of the same faith (we had met as new teachers at the same high school). For about five years, there was an extraordinary wholeness in my life. There was a single, unifying spiritual focus that included my marriage, my participation in a local community of faith, my professional work, my writing, my closest friends and relatives.

This degree of unity in my life came to a gradual end after I was laid off as part of a downsizing/restructuring that the church organization underwent. The period between jobs was actually a time of marked spiritual growth. One thing that was clear throughout was that I was seeking work with a sense of purpose, an opportunity to serve the greater good of humanity. When I accepted an offer from a nonprofit organization (the Institute for Responsive Education) devoted to the reform of K-12 education, with an emphasis on achieving equity through family-school-community collaboration, I felt that my prayers had been answered.

Nevertheless, I found a kind of dualism creeping into my life. Here's part of what went into my journal about twelve years later, on December 21, 2001, when I had read most of *The Courage to Teach* (Palmer 1998):

I read Parker Palmer and I find myself asking, What happened? It was always my intention to lead a career that was spiritually informed and lit up and so to lead an undivided life. But I find that my life, while by no means hermetically sealed in its compartmentalization, nonetheless falls short of my own longstanding ideal of an undivided life. My essential life of spiritual study and growth, of poetry and intuition is at too much of a distance from my professional writing, work, and thinking

. . . It is time now to recommit to a life undivided. It is time to demonstrate the courage to live my deepest convictions throughout my life.

I won't try to capture all the subtle ways that my inner struggle began to move me a little closer to my ideal. Instead, I'll jump to September 2002, when I picked up the new issue of *The School Administrator* and was delighted to see that it was entirely focused on "Spirituality in Leadership." In his introductory essay, Paul Houston noted that in his speeches he began talking about the spiritual nature of educators' work:

"Then a funny thing happened on the way to the controversy I antici-pated. Rather than creating protest, this became the one part of what I was saying that prompted the most follow up and support. Clearly, a hunger in our midst exists for finding our deeper purpose and for con-ducting our work in a more enlightened manner" (2002, 6).

When I read those words, it was as though a light switched on in my consciousness. I had been feeling for some time that a book might be a natural next step in my work, but I suddenly realized what such a book could explore. Ideas and themes for a book on the spiritual dimension of leading educational progress began forming quickly and effortlessly and with a wonderful sense of energy. Frank Duffy, the editor of the se-ries that this book is a part of, had already suggested that I submit a book proposal, but it was only at this point that I had the clarity of di-rection and commitment needed to answer that call.

NOTES

1. William Stafford died in 1993, but I shared this poem with his protégé, the poet Naomi Shihab Nye, and she sent it along to Kim Stafford, William's son.
2. http://csf.colorado.edu/sine/transcripts/palmer.html.

REFERENCES

Houston, P. D. (2002). "Why Spirituality and Why Now?" *The School Admin-istrator* 59, no. 8 (September): 6–8.

Palmer, P. J. (1998). *The Courage to Teach: Exploring the Inner Landscape of a Teacher's Life.* San Francisco: Jossey-Bass.

———. (n.d.). "The Grace of Great Things: Recovering the Sacred in Know-ing, Teaching, and Learning." http://csf.colorado.edu/sine/transcripts/palmer.html

Stafford, W. (1993). "Ask Me." *The Darkness around Us Is Deep: Selected Poems of William Stafford.* New York: HarperPerennial.

Acknowledgments

I am triply indebted to Sophie Sa, the founding executive director of the Panasonic Foundation. First, in an act of extraordinary generosity and support, she, as my boss at Panasonic, allowed me to devote nearly one-fifth (a day each week) of my salaried time to researching and writing this book. Further, in what felt to me like a strong vote of confidence, this time was given without strings attached; this time was not given in exchange for the inclusion or exclusion of any particular content.

Second, Sophie read and commented on an early draft of the book. Her candid and insightful response was invaluable.

Third, for eight years I have been privileged to work closely with Sophie as Panasonic Foundation's assistant director. While her influence on my development as thinker, researcher, writer, and student of educational change and leadership would be impossible to quantify, suffice it to say that it has been immensely beneficial.

It's essential to acknowledge that the foundation would not have been the kind of nurturing and stimulating place it has been if Sophie and her staff had not been guided and supported by a board of directors that is at once distinguished and sympathetic. In addition to Sophie, the current board comprises Robert Ingersoll (Chair), Robert Greenberg, Paul Liao, Deborah Meier, Martin Meyerson, and Ira Perlman. Board secretary Sandra Karriem, who is a Panasonic attorney, generously advised me on the contract for this book.

My development as a student of educational change and leadership has also benefitted considerably from my work with Panasonic Foundation's senior consultants (some of whom are now doing other things): Dean Damon, LaVaun Dennett, Scott Elliff, Lawrence Feldman, Stephen Fink, David Florio, Gail Gerry, Andrew Gelber, JoAnn Heryla, Sue Kinzer, Lallie Lloyd, Fern Mann, Patricia Mitchell, George Perry, Tony Rollins, Gladys Sheehan, Kenneth J. Tewel, Betty Jo Webb, and Deborah Winking.

The book would simply not be what it is without the contributions of the seventeen people, most of whom are or have been educational leaders, who generously allowed me to interview them in depth. The insights they offered from their life experiences as educational leaders and spiritual practitioners constitute an enormous contribution to the substance of this book. They are Les Adelson, Brian Benzel, LaVaun Dennett, Larry Feldman, Steve Fink, Carl Glickman, JoAnn Heryla, Carol Johnson, John Kammerud, Larry Leverett, Cheri Lovre, Timothy Lucas, John Morefield, Les Omotani, Fred Stokley, Louise Sundin, and Betty Jo Webb. Each one of these individuals, even those who are not directly quoted in the book, inspired and informed my thinking in ways that were invaluable.

I am also indebted to Francis Duffy, the editor of the series of which this book is a part. Frank invited me to submit a book proposal before the idea for this book had been formulated. Later, when I came to him with my idea, and at every step of the process thereafter, Frank has been a wonderful support and a valuable advisor.

I am deeply grateful to the following people who took the time and care to read and comment on the manuscript and whose observations helped me bring the book to final form: David Andrews, Frank Duffy, Steve Fink, Sophie Sa, Taffy Thompson, and June Thompson.

I am humbled and thrilled that this book includes a foreword by Meg Wheatley, whose pioneering work, exploring the interstices between new developments in science and organizational leadership, has been inspiring and energizing my thinking for years.

I am thankful to Tom Koerner, Cindy Tursman, and the rest of the crew at Rowman & Littlefield Education who shepherded the book from manuscript to final, printed form.

My thanks also to Thomas Wilson, who, upon learning of my work on this book, recommended Derrick Bell's *Ethical Ambition;* this proved to be a valuable source, especially for the chapter entitled "Moral Purpose, Moral Passion, Moral Courage."

A book of this sort is shaped in part by who the author is. In this regard, I want to express my profound gratitude to my parents, sisters, wife, daughter, and close friends David and Joan Andrews, Howard ("Stu") Stewart, David Wilck, Bradwell D. Scott, and many, many others for relationships that have made all the difference.

I am happy for this opportunity to express my deep thanks to Allison W. Phinney Jr., who is my spiritual teacher. In 1984, I took a two-week course of intensive spiritual study and instruction with him, and the impact of that experience on my spiritual growth and development would be impossible to overstate. Since then I have attended full-day annual meetings that he conducts for all of his students and have benefited from conversations, correspondence, articles he has written, and the radiance of his example of living spiritually in a world that relentlessly tugs in a very different direction.

My humble and immense thanks to one and all.

CHAPTER 1

Introduction: Spiritual Leadership for Improving Public Schools

9/11. How powerful those two numbers together have become. They evoke a devastating and world-altering event. The event itself was incomprehensibly horrific, shocking in its brutal exploitation of the vulnerabilities of an open society. And yet that same event quickly became the source of a resurgence of spirit. It shook people to the core, and when they were shaken they saw more clearly what matters most—what gives meaning to life.

It was not only that the stark evil and wanton destructiveness of the suicidal assaults on the World Trade Center and the Pentagon repelled us to the opposite of evil and destruction, although that is certainly part of what was going on. We were also profoundly moved by the courageous self-sacrifice of firefighters, police officers, emergency workers, airline crews and passengers, and others, and those heroic acts stood in bold contrast to the barbaric hatefulness of the attacks. But that, too, only partially explains our response.

An important part of what was shattered that day—at least for a time—was an often shallow, isolated, self-serving, and materialistic approach to living. Underneath that patina we recognized again a profound need for connection and meaning. We called the people we loved, and we reconnected with feelings and places within ourselves that are too easily buried under quotidian details.

This change of consciousness was expressed in a *New York Times* editorial shortly before the first anniversary of 9/11, which included the following:

> New Yorkers have never looked at one another the way they did that
> morning and in the days following. There's no need to exaggerate the

bond that arose in this city as the towers came down and the stark realization set in. If you were there, you'll remember that sense of collective focus, that clinging together, as vividly as the clouds of
powdered concrete and smoke that filled the air. That coherence, amid
so much incoherence, persisted for days and then weeks. . . . That
unity, that clinging together was the only joy to be found, but it was,
in its way, a profound joy, amid profound grief. (*New York Times* 2002,
A22)

Almost a year before—one week after 9/11/2001—a *Times* editorial
included this:

The tragedy at the World Trade Center has produced scores of stories
about people whose cool heads and courage saved lives. Among them are
the public-school teachers who evacuated several schools that were dan-
gerously near the collapsing towers and moved a total of 8,000 children
to safety without a single serious injury. Their achievement is all the
more amazing given that the disaster struck on the third day of the school
year, requiring many teachers to deal with frightened children whom
they hardly knew.

. . . The teachers at Public School 234, on Chambers Street, had to
evacuate 6 and 7 year olds during the most harrowing part of the disaster, just after the second trade center tower collapsed, enveloping the
school in a debris-filled cloud.

Many of the children were screaming for parents who actually worked
in the towers. . . . Taking some students by the hand and carrying others
on their shoulders, the teachers plunged through rubble-strewn streets
that were clogged with adults running for their lives.

The editorial concludes: "Parents and city officials should be grate-
ful for the poise and calm with which the public-school teachers of
Lower Manhattan handled a life-threatening situation" (*New York
Times* 2001).

This editorial is first and foremost about the qualities exhibited by
the particular teachers in an extreme emergency. But to me it also
says something more. It speaks to the qualities of teachers and educational leaders all across the United States, as well as in other coun-
tries. It's a unique profession that attracts unique people. People in
this profession devote themselves to the safety of the students in their

care. But, of course, there's even more: They have a shaping influence that will affect how students use their minds and hearts during their whole lives.

In another regard, educators and educational leaders share a widespread need with the rest of humanity. It's a deep-down desire to live lives and develop careers that are meaningful—connected to a higher purpose. This desire can all too easily get hidden in the hustle and clamor of life in the twenty-first century. The desire for connection to a higher purpose too often gets muffled or even silenced by "the deafening electronic roar of commercialism without meaningful human content" (Louv 1995, 55). If there's any message at all to be wrested from the commercial roar, it's that your purpose in life is to be a successful consumer. And that, of course, is not a higher purpose or a purpose with any meaning at all.

Educational leaders have learned that the desire for connection to a higher purpose can also be bruised and humiliated by the social complexities and political intensity of leading a public school or school system through fundamental changes. And yet that deep-lying desire may be essential to sustainable progress in public education. For, as Allison W. Phinney points out, "the traditional narrow focus of most leaders in seeking primarily outward economic and social improvements offers little hope of stirring human beings increasingly dispirited by pervasive materialism. And without humanity's morale or will to sustain outward social improvements, they are negated by shifting circumstances and deteriorating attitudes" (2003, 238).

And this brings us to the subject of this book: spiritual leadership for systemic school improvement. Our public school systems must be transformed to realize much more of the fullness of their purpose to help every child who comes to school realize his or her intellectual, social, creative, and moral potential. It is my contention that the level of educational progress that is now needed will not be realized without a fuller understanding and practice of the spiritual dimensions of educational leadership. The problems we face in public education cannot be tackled through a singular reliance on the resources of personal ego and objectivist assumptions. A materialistic mind-set shuts out the deeper powers and possibilities for advances in education. Spiritual leadership is indispensable.

A materialist might say that the spiritual dimensions of educational leadership might be more to the point if they weren't so elusive. But a great deal of what profoundly matters in this world *cannot* be perceived from a strictly materialistic or sensory standpoint. How important are the following—love, justice, truth, hope, freedom, wholeness, identity, order, inspiration, honor, glory, trust, intuition, beauty, purpose, vision, meaning, principle, joy, spirit, grace, sacrifice, generosity, gratitude, courage, commitment, openness, soul?

Who could imagine—much less bear to live in—a world where everything on that list was somehow completely and permanently wiped out? And how different would human experience be with the total loss of even one of these dimension-opening essentials? So much of what matters most in our lives and in our work cannot be seen, touched, tasted, heard, or smelled.

In a speech to the United States Congress, former Czech president Václav Havel remarked on what matters most: "Consciousness precedes being, and not the other way around, as the Marxists claim. For this reason, the salvation of this world lies nowhere else than in the human heart, in the human power to reflect, in human meekness and in human responsibility. Without a global revolution in the sphere of human consciousness, nothing will change for the better in the sphere of our being as humans" (quoted in Palmer 1990).

Parker Palmer comments: "Matter, [Havel] is trying to tell us, is not the fundamental factor in the movement of history. Spirit is. Consciousness is. Human awareness is. Thought is. Spirituality is. Those are the deep sources of freedom and power with which people have been able to move boulders and create change" (1990).

Spiritual leadership is the heart of leadership. We can find in it the power to move boulders that have made progress in systemic educational change so painstakingly slow.

WHAT SPIRITUAL LEADERSHIP IS AND IS NOT

First, a few words on what spiritual leadership is not. It's not holier-than-thou, head-in-the-clouds, mysterious, unaccountable, ethereal, pious, jargon-thick syrup. Nor is it sectarian dogmatism or a subtle new way to desecularize schools and get religion back into the class-room.

Spirituality is a state of mind or consciousness that enables one to perceive deeper levels of experience, meaning, values, and purpose than can be perceived from a strictly materialistic vantage point. *Spiritual leadership*, then, is leading from those deeper levels.

For some individuals, spiritual leadership may have roots in a particular religious tradition. The spirituality of others will be rooted in nonreligious or syncretic soil. It seems important to me that those whose convictions have been denominationally shaped should not wear their religion on their sleeves — at least not on the job in a public school district. This is not an argument for hiding one's spiritual light under a bushel, but it is an argument for recognizing a sharp distinction between subtle or not-so-subtle sectarian proselytizing and genuine spiritual leadership. And it is an argument for recognizing the critical importance of the wall of separation between church and state.

At the same time, it's important that in our zeal to maintain the strength of this wall we not violate "the deepest needs of the human soul," as Palmer points out (1998/1999, 6). I endorse these words of Carol Johnson, superintendent of Memphis Public Schools:

> I think that public education has worked so hard for many decades to separate church and state to create this sort of neutral place where children of all faiths could feel safe and welcome that to some extent we've also negated the fact that our children and families live in communities that include their having spiritual experiences that are really connected to a deeper sense of who they are and where they fit in the world. I feel that the balance we have to create here is to have enough neutrality to say "you will not be treated differently" or "you will not be valued more or less based on what your spiritual identity is," but that still affirms your right to have that spiritual identity and to speak to it and talk about it in ways that aren't negating others' spiritual home or spiritual connection.[1]

It is helpful in this context to distinguish spirituality from institutional religion, the former being broadly inclusive in its transcendence of denominational doctrine and practice (Houston 2002). What flows through the world's diversity of religions and in the hearts and souls of spiritual leaders and practitioners is the spiritual energy that awakens consciousness to deeper levels of experience, purpose, values, and meaning than can be perceived from a strictly materialistic vantage point. Spiritual leadership means leading from those deeper levels, and it is the purposeful actions and behaviors that naturally follow from doing so.

ANOTHER BOOK ON LEADERSHIP?

The world is flooded with books and articles on leadership, and the river of new books and articles feeding this flood shows no signs of abatement. Given the plethora of such books, I'm feeling the need to justify this one. If this book was focused on leadership writ large, or even educational leadership broadly considered, I would have a difficult time making a case for a new one.

Spiritual leadership has received considerably less attention, and spiritual leadership for progress in the systemic reform of public education is not the subject of many books. Yet the *work* of spiritual leadership for systemic progress in public education—which is essentially invisible—is very much going on. And this brings us to the purpose of—and justification for—this book. The intent is to make new connections within the education reform movement; specifically, to make visible an aspect of the movement that is generally invisible. In expressing the natural power of self-connection, Margaret Wheatley draws on the image of a spider, who does not abandon but reweaves her web when it is broken:

> The most profound strategy for changing a living network comes from biology, although we could learn it directly from a spider. If a system is in trouble, it can be restored to health by connecting it more to itself. . . . If a system is suffering, this indicates that it lacks sufficient access to itself. It might be lacking information, it might have lost clarity about who it is, it might have troubled relationships, it might be ignoring those who have valuable insights. (1999, 145)

My approach in researching this book has been to explore some of what is emerging and developing in the area of spiritual leadership for educational progress by delving into the surrounding literature and conducting in-depth interviews with educational leaders. By interweaving what I have discovered in the literature and interviews, I attempt in this book to connect readers to their own field in ways that might open new perspectives and unleash new energies. By seeking to make what has been invisible more visible—namely, the spiritual dimensions of educational leadership—the book aspires to connect its readers to the fullness of what is spiritually possible in education.

OVERVIEW OF THE BOOK

Each of the following chapters explores a particular theme—a dimension of spiritual leadership for whole-system educational transformation. What follows here is a very brief summation of these themes.

Wholeness and Whole-System Transformation

This chapter first defines and offers a rationale for *whole-system educational transformation*, and then explores its interrelationship with systems thinking and with the spiritual, philosophical, and scientific conviction that wholeness underlies the surface illusion of fragmentation.

Called to Serve

Educational work is a call to service, and service is the heart of educational leadership. This chapter explores the concept of servant-leadership in the context of whole-system educational transformation.

Habits of Spiritual Leaders

The spiritual dimensions of educational leadership are scarcely discernible, much less nourished, in the social upheaval and political turmoil that fundamental reform arouses. In such an environment, a spiritual perspective can only be gained through the disciplined development of spiritual practices.

Groundwork: Trust, Openness, and Ownership

The foundation for sustainable change in education involves three closely related essentials: trust, openness, and ownership. Trust engenders openness, and openness invites connections, and connections stimulate the innovation that is essential to whole system change in public education.

Groundwork: The Power of Vision and the Anchor of Core Values

The daunting challenges that leaders of educational change face in the twenty-first century simply cannot be met without the transforming power of shared vision and the anchoring influence of broadly owned core values.

Case Study: Transforming a School System

The role of spiritual leadership in transforming organizational culture as a foundation for whole-system educational improvement is explored in this case study of Edmonds School District, near Seattle. Think of this case study as an instantiation of the themes the previous two chapters explore.

Moral Purpose, Moral Passion, Moral Courage

Moral purpose, passion, and courage are indispensable, because nothing less can answer the urgent need for progress in creating and sustaining systems of education that enable *all* children to receive a high-quality education.

Eye of the Storm, or Clarity in Chaos

Reform leadership in public education is tumultuous work that produces storms of various kinds. It's probably not possible to lead from outside these storms. This chapter looks at the experience of leaders who have located the eyes of storms they have found themselves in. In other words, they have found a place of clarity in the stir of organizational upheaval and led from that inner place.

"What Power Had I Before I Learned to Yield?"

This chapter explores the following questions: If the notion of controlling something as complex as a public school system is actually an illusion, is there power to be found in moving beyond that illusion? If so, what sort of power is that, and what is a leader's role in relation to it?

Humility in High Places

The most successful leaders are powerfully focused on, and relentlessly committed to, something much larger than their egos and self interests. Humility frees leaders and spiritual practitioners from the blinding influence of egotism.

A Vision: Educational Rain Forests

I leave the reader with a personal vision for education.

The use of thematic chapters is a way to organize and contain what would otherwise expand into an amorphous immensity that no book could hold. But the subject does not permit a strict separation into thematic domains. Rather, the themes regularly infiltrate each other's territory. They are so intricately intertwined that their recurrence from beginning to end cannot be suppressed, regardless of an author's desire for tidy segmentation.

A FEW CAVEATS

Spiritual leadership may be the heart of leadership, but that's not to say that it is the whole of it. This book is not designed to be a complete guide to leading systemic educational change (nor for that matter is it a complete guide to spiritual leadership, a subject whose dimensions are beyond the scope of this one volume). There are a great number of instrumental, structural, and political aspects to systemic educational leadership that the successful system-level leader must attend to but that receive scant attention here because they are, at most, tangentially related to spiritual leadership.

At the same time, it's important to acknowledge that some of what is included in these pages is not the exclusive domain of spiritual leadership. The groundwork chapters, for example, explore subjects — trust, openness, ownership, vision, and values — that systemic reformers who may see no connections between spirituality and their work in education would also include in their descriptions of successfully reforming school systems. These themes fall within the broad definition of spirituality that I am using for the purposes of this book, but the same themes can be approached from different angles, using different lenses.

This book draws on an array of previously published works and from seventeen original interviews. It represents a wide range of perspectives and spiritual orientations. Some views included in this book contradict other views that I have included. While it would theoretically have been possible to polish the material drawn from the various sources in an effort to make the argument more seamless, I have not been inclined to do so. Such an approach could not have been fully true to the sources or to the diversity of perspectives that I believe provides a truer picture of where this germinal movement, if it can be even accurately called a movement, now stands.

At the same time, it's important to say that this book is not a neutral survey of "what's out there." While I've occasionally included quotations from published works and interviews that I am not in complete agreement with, it's also true that I came to this task with a point of view and have shaped the material according to particular convictions and predilections concerning systemic educational improvement, leadership, and spirituality.

NOTE

1. Carol Johnson was superintendent of Minneapolis Public Schools when I interviewed her for this book.

REFERENCES

Houston, D. (2002). "Why Spirituality, and Why Now?" *The School Administrator,* September, 6–8.

Louv, R. (1995). The New Culture of Renewal. *New Schools, New Communities* 11, no. 3 (Spring): 55.

New York Times. September 18, 2001.

———. September 9, 2002. "New York, a Year Later: Things Regained, Things Lost," A22.

Palmer, P. (1990). "Leading from Within." www.teacherformation.org/html/rr/leading.cfm?dep_mode=print.

———. (1998/1999). "Evoking the Spirit in Public Education." *Educational Leadership* 56, no. 4 (December-January): 6–11.

Phinney, A. W. (2003). "The Dynamic Now—A Poet's Counsel." In B. S. Baudot, ed., *Candles in the Dark: A New Spirit for a Plural World.* Manchester: New Hampshire Institute of Politics at Saint Anselm College.

Wheatley, M. J. (1999). *Leadership and the New Science: Discovering Order in a Chaotic World.* 2d ed. San Francisco: Berrett-Koehler.

CHAPTER 2

Wholeness and
Whole-System Transformation

Too few children in too many public schools receive the quality of education needed to live and work successfully in a full-throttle world. Furthermore, children of color and children in poverty are too often marooned in low-performing schools. The imperative to provide all students with a high-quality education is moral even more than it is economic. Given what we know of the enduring consequences for individuals of educational starvation — not to mention the cost to society and democracy — providing a high-quality education for all children is quite simply the right thing to do (Thompson 2001).

We know of good schools that are succeeding with students deemed least likely to succeed: students of color and students in poverty.[1] But in a nation of 50 million schoolchildren, we face an enormous, yet-to-be-met challenge: namely, taking such success to scale. The one-school-here-and-another-there approach to educational reform sidesteps the reality that schools thrive, fail, or stumble along in the context of social and educational systems. The quality of those systems exerts enormous influence over the quality of the schools within them.

For several decades, school-by-school reforms in education predominated. Consider the Coalition of Essential Schools, Accelerated Schools, or James Comer's School Development Program in its first several decades. That movement became increasingly holistic in its philosophy and approach — at least at the school level. Reformers came to recognize that the school must be treated as a complete system, and that piecemeal reforms — a classroom here, a curricular change there — are doomed to short-lived success or to none at all.

Over time one can see the emergence of an expanding recognition that the web of interrelationships that make a school a whole system extend well beyond the school. For a public school, this wider web includes parents and community, other schools in the same system, system-level leaders and staff, including the school board, the leaders of various unions or associations, the superintendent and her or his cabinet, and an array of staff members who make up the central office.

This web of interconnections is dynamically complex—multifaceted and ever changing. A school district's organization chart, for example, may be static and well ordered on paper, but it becomes fluid in reality as school and district administrators, board members, teachers, students, parents, and community and union leaders act, react, and interact; as unpredictable events occur; and as the unintended consequences of carefully planned actions unfold (Thompson 2003a).

For all the fluidity and dynamism of school districts as social systems, the fundamental features of their underlying culture and structure tend to be stubbornly inert. It's a well-known fact that the modern public school and school district are direct descendants of the Industrial Revolution. Public schools were modeled after factories, and factories were built to last. Factories have traditionally been designed with an eye toward optimizing efficiency through regimented processes. A blood relative of such regimentation is aversion to change.

Given the double-barreled challenge of social flux and bureaucratic intransigence, it's no wonder that those involved in efforts to transform factory-style school districts into adaptive, high-performing systems of education have experienced such tough sledding and demonstrated only spotty progress. At the same time, it's important to recognize and learn from early successes in whole-system educational improvement efforts.

There is a simple theory of change (one that I hold in common with my colleagues at the Panasonic Foundation) that accompanies efforts toward whole-system educational improvement: If your aim is to improve student learning across the board, then you must improve schools across the board. But if those schools are part of a system of schools, their improvement will not be sustainable unless the system as a whole is transformed. More specifically, it's essential to transform our factory-modeled command-and-control bureaucracies into high-performance systems of education, systems where individuals and teams work in concert throughout the organization around shared purpose, values, and vision.

SYSTEMS THINKING

Successful whole-system improvement of public education is contingent on leaders' ability to think and act systemically, and by that I mean not only understanding the need for system-wide change, but also perceiving the dynamics at work in complex systems. The disciplines of organizational learning—systems thinking being chief among them—comprise a powerful set of concepts and tools for uncovering the underlying dynamics that cause complex human systems, such as school districts and multinational corporations, to behave the way they do (Thompson 2003b). This way of thinking and taking action has been evolving over many decades, but it reached its widest audience with the publication of *The Fifth Discipline* by Peter Senge (1990).

Among the systems thinking tools are systems archetypes, which are patterns of counterproductive organizational behavior that are repeated in diverse contexts. Because these patterns play out under the surface, they are seldom recognized, so people and organizations are essentially doomed to blindly repeat them, unless they develop the ability to discern underlying patterns and to probe into their cultural and systemic sources. Systems theorists have identified at least a dozen systems archetypes (Senge 1990, 94–113 and 378–90; Senge et al. 1994, 121–50).

One of the archetypes is called "Shifting the Burden." Daniel Kim, publisher of *The Systems Thinker*, uses an aspect of the Helen Keller story to illustrate this archetype (1992). Because of her blindness and deafness, Keller's parents had a tendency to rush to her aid with every problem she faced, and it's easy enough to sympathize with their inclination to help their daughter. But Keller may never have realized her potential had another person, with a very different approach, not become a part of her story. Keller's teacher, Ann Sullivan, saw that she and the parents must not allow her student's disabilities to prevent Keller from becoming self-reliant. Keller, of course, went on to graduate from Radcliffe College and to become an author and role model for people with disabilities and for many others.

Kim explains, "Helen Keller's story is much more than an inspirational human interest story; it illustrates a pervasive dynamic that is rooted in an archetypal structure. The well-intentioned actions of her parents shifted the burden of responsibility for Helen's welfare to them" (22).

Shifting the burden takes place when an obvious "solution" is used to relieve what is perceived as a problem but is actually only a symptom of the problem. Kim observes that "these symptomatic solutions have two specific negative effects. First, they divert attention away from the real or fundamental source of the problem. More subtly, symptomatic solutions cause the viability of the fundamental solution to deteriorate over time, reinforcing the perceived need for more of the symptomatic solution" (22). Shifting the burden, in other words, is an approach that employs short-term remedies *at the expense* of long-term solutions.

Let's apply the archetype to one of the most prominent features on the contemporary educational landscape: high-stakes, standardized test-based accountability policies and practices. Shifting the burden, like all the systems archetypes, is a tool for probing assumptions. What are the assumptions at work in high-stakes, test-based accountability? It is assumed, correctly I believe, that on the whole—and most acutely in areas of concentrated poverty—our public schools are not enabling students to achieve at levels that will assure their success in life and work.

It is further assumed that the basic problem is low test scores, or, if not the scores themselves, then a level of learning that can best be tracked by test scores. Other assumptions flow from these. If the problem is best described by low test scores, then we need regular testing both to spur and to monitor results on standardized tests. A whole system of accountability is then built around test scores.

The trouble is that the burden is being shifted. Test scores are the symptom, not the underlying problem. And while strategies aimed at raising test scores may result in higher test scores, the unintended consequences of this symptomatic "solution" will, in the long run, I believe, be harmful, if not toxic, to schools and students. High-stakes, test-based accountability assumes that higher test scores equal better learning, but researchers have found that it is possible to raise test scores without improving the quality of teaching and learning in the classroom (Kohn 2001, McNeil 2000, Schemo and Fessenden 2003). In fact, it is possible to raise test scores by lowering the quality of teaching and learning.

The situation is perhaps analogous to farmers being rewarded or punished according to the annual weight of their animals. If the stakes were high enough, farmers would find ways to boost animal weight prior to the annual "weigh-in." It is not difficult to imagine how the short-term success of tactics for increasing animal weight could have deadly long-term effects both on the animals and farm productivity.

So, if low test scores are symptoms and not the underlying problem, then what is the "real" problem? The fundamental challenge in public education, it seems to me, is that our nation is now calling upon our systems of education to accomplish a goal that these systems were never designed to address. For much of the twentieth century, our factory-modeled school systems carried out their purpose of sorting and separating high achievers from low achievers. But the goal now is to enable all students—students across the socioeconomic, racial, and ethnic spectrum—to graduate from high school prepared for college-level work or living-wage jobs in a world of constant change. How can this goal be achieved without systematically and systemically building the capacities of educators and educational leaders to accomplish what has never previously been accomplished in public education?

Meeting this challenge in our nation's ninety-four thousand schools will require educational leaders to move beyond the old notion that educational performance can be mechanistically controlled. It will also require leaders to confront what Senge terms organizational *learning disabilities* (1990, 17). Recognizing and redressing these *disabilities* can be an important step toward developing the capacity to undertake and sustain systemwide changes aimed at improving student and school performance.

Learning disabilities that plague school systems, adapted in part from Senge (1990, 17–26), include the following:

Narrow Job or Role Definition and Compartmentalized Structure

Most districts are organized into departments (Thompson 1999). This fosters compartmentalization and a limited view of whole-system issues, needs, and concerns (Fink and Thompson 2001). This in turn works against organizational flexibility and a culture of collaboration around a common purpose.

Blame Shifting

Compartmentalized structure and narrow role definitions feed the tendency to shift blame to another person or department. Until individuals see the larger system and their place within that system, it will be difficult for them to assume responsibility for addressing problems within their sphere of influence and within the system at large.

Staring at Events but Missing the Patterns

When a crisis erupts in a school or central office, we tend to look for the immediate "cause," put out that "fire," and then go on to the next one. This is where system archetypes such as shifting the burden and other systems tools come in. A key reason that symptoms get mistaken for causes is that, in complex systems, cause and effect are often separated by considerable distance in time and space. A board policy in 2003 can give rise to a dispute between teachers and parents in a particular school in 2005, but the relationship between the two would only be evident after a thoughtful probing into underlying cultural or structural realities. By developing a long, whole-system view, educational leaders can learn to see trends and patterns that point to invisible systemic causes. As superintendent Les Omotani explains, "The systems thinking approach offers the chance to deal with the real genesis of problems and seize opportunities you might not be able to otherwise get a hold of. Do you go to the headwaters and divert the river, or do you just wait for the flood?" (quoted in Thompson 1999, 2).

The Illusion of Taking Charge

Our conceptions of leadership and management tend to be deeply influenced by the "lone ranger" myth of the hero who single-handedly takes control and solves difficult challenges. These conceptions lead to such ironic and impractical—but nevertheless widespread—practices as mandating site-based decision making. But as Michael Fullan points out, "You Can't Mandate What Matters (The more complex the change the less you can force it)" (1993). Leading a school system through the complexities of change involves the development of shared ownership around a common purpose and vision (topics that I explore in depth in later chapters). Such an approach taps into energies and potentials that are wholly inaccessible to command-and-control leaders.

Whole-system change in education is not simply school reform on a wider scale. It requires the leader to make a quantum leap from the school district as a manageable machine to the school district as a living system—complex and dynamic—as something comparable to an ecosystem with its webs of fluid interrelationships and evolving interdependencies. Making this leap involves a change of consciousness so that the leader is focused less on externals than on the invisible forces at work at a deep level.

TUNING INTO THE ENCOMPASSING, UNFOLDING ORDER

Answerers

> There are songs too wide for sound. There are quiet
> places where something stopped a long time
> ago and the days began to open
> their mouths toward nothing but the sky. We live
> in place of the many who stir only
> if we listen, only because the living
> live and call out. I am ready
> as all of us are who wake at night:
> we become rooms for whatever almost
> is. It speaks in us, trying. And even if
> only by a note like this, we answer.
>
> —William Stafford

Learning to "answer," to respond to a dimension that is wider and deeper than what the senses register, is an aspect of leadership that has received limited attention in the leadership literature and seminars. Yet this ability may be central to the realization of the full potential of educational leadership for whole-system transformation.

"When you open your soul and when you bring your whole heart into the room, it changes the structure of the room," says Joseph Jaworski, founder of the American Leadership Forum and cofounder of Generon Consulting (as quoted in Scharmer 2000, 38). William Stafford's words apply not only to poets. Spiritual leaders "become rooms for whatever almost is"; they become receivers and containers of a reality that unfolds in ways that can be intuited but never forced.

Artists and athletes have sometimes been able to come into rapport with invisible forces that are larger than themselves. Consider legendary basketball star Bill Russell's description along these lines:

> Every so often a Celtics game would heat up so that it became more than a physical or even a mental game, and would be magical. That feeling is very difficult to describe, and I certainly never talked about it when I was playing. When it happened, I could feel my play rise to a new level. It came rarely and would last anywhere from five minutes to a whole quarter or more. . . . It would surround not only me and the other Celtics, but also the players on the other team, even the referees.
>
> At that special level, all sorts of odd things happened. The game would be in a white heat of competition, and yet somehow I wouldn't feel competitive—which is a miracle in itself. I'd be putting out the maximum effort, straining, coughing up parts of my lungs as we ran, and yet I never felt the pain. The game would move so quickly that every fake, cut and pass would be surprising, and yet nothing could surprise me. It was almost as if we were playing in slow motion. During those spells, I could almost sense how the next play would develop and where the next shot would be taken. . . . My premonitions would be consistently correct, and I always felt then that I not only knew all of the Celtics by heart, but also the opposing players, and that they all knew me. There have been many times in my career when I felt moved or joyful, but these were the moments when I had chills pulsing up and down my spine. (Quoted in Jaworski 1996, 54–55).

Russell, it seems to me, gives new meaning to the term "high performance." Perhaps when we speak of a high-performance organization or system what we have in our heads is something like a well-oiled machine. But what Russell is talking about involves a profound responsiveness or yielding to a truth beyond the senses. Jaworski puts it this way:

"Once we see ourselves as part of the unfolding, creative order in life, we can sense what is wanting to emerge, and take an active role in shaping the future" (1999). The most powerful and sustainable progress in changing institutions will result not from willful efforts to plan, control, determine, and push forward, but from a profound openness of heart and mind that allows more powerful possibilities to unfold.

This kind of leadership requires faith, patience, intuition, humility, expectancy, inspiration, and, yes, spirituality. We tend to be heavily reliant on physical sense perceptions and rationality, "but why assume that sensation and rationality are the only points of correspondence between the human self and the world?" asks Parker Palmer. "Why assume so, when the human self is rich with other capacities—intuition, empathy, emotion, and faith, to name but a few? If there is nothing to be known by these faculties, why do we have them? . . . We ourselves are part of the reality we wish to know: does the multiplicity of our modes of knowing suggest a similar multiplicity in the nature of that reality?" (1993, 53).

It is through spiritual sensing, listening, and seeing that our perception and experience of reality—of how it works and what is possible—changes, opens up (Kahane 2001, 25). I had an experience not long ago that suggests to me a relationship between creativity, receptivity, and a kind of heightened or expanded perception. On a Saturday afternoon in January, I took a hike down a mountainside to a frozen lake. On the hike back up the mountain, going by a different route, I came upon a partially frozen-over stream, where I stopped, took my camera from my knapsack, and shot a few photos.

Then as I walked on, I realized something that I've experienced before but perhaps had never consciously considered. After taking a few pictures—after making those creative decisions—I was *seeing* more. Instead of merely passing through a static landscape, now I was experiencing a richly nuanced world in something closer to its fullness. Instead of walking by cold and inert material surfaces, I discovered myself in a place that was dimensionally alive and then I was sensing that the true energy of the place had nothing to do with material surfaces and everything to do with spiritual subterrain.

The act of hiking alone in the woods had involved a slowing of my pace and a growing receptivity. Then when I began taking pictures, a certain creative energy was released. With the fusion of receptivity and creativity, I became more awake, more attuned to the surrounding forest. As a result, I literally saw more of what was around me, but I also felt an energy that I had not sensed in the previous hour of hiking.

This experience was subjective. I felt the forest's vitality within. In that experience, I was no longer separate, but at one with the place. I experienced myself in its wholeness.

VISIBLE FRAGMENTATION, INVISIBLE WHOLENESS

There is a path which no fowl knoweth, and which the vulture's eye hath not seen.

—Job

Now faith is substance of things hoped for, the evidence of things not seen.

—Paul

Oh, hidden deep but ever present!

—Lao Tsu

What is originality? To see something that has no name as yet and hence cannot be mentioned though it stares us all in the face. The way men usually are, it takes a name to make something visible for them.

—Friedrich Nietzsche

As mortals gain more correct views of God and man, multitudinous objects of creation, which before were invisible, will become visible.

—Mary Baker Eddy

We once were made secure by things visible, by structures we could see. Now it is time to embrace the invisible.

—Margaret J. Wheatley

Educational leaders are daily surrounded by mountains of evidence suggesting they are living and working in a world of fragmentation, of disconnection and missed connections. The events, encounters, issues, and actions that make up any given day on the job feel like fallen leaves in a shifting breeze, or to put it more crassly: like one damn thing after another. Educational leaders regularly see people and groups of people working at cross purposes when it was never their intention to do so. Educational leaders put out "fires," go to meetings, answer hordes of e-mails, and struggle to implement externally imposed mandates and regulations.

Whole-system approaches to educational improvement promise to bring a measure of coherence and unity to this work. And systems thinking offers important concepts and tools for getting underneath the surface of events and addressing root causes. Both spiritual traditions and contemporary scientific discoveries suggest that at a deep invisible level, wholeness is the nature of reality itself, and that what we experience as fragmentation is an illusion or misperception.

David Bohm was a leading physicist and theorist of the twentieth century who worked with Einstein and various pioneers of the quantum revolution. He was also inspired by mysticism and made contact with both J. Krishnamurti and the Dalai Lama. His book *Wholeness and the Implicate Order* includes the following observations:

> Fragmentation is now very widespread, not only throughout society, but also in each individual; and this is leading to a kind of general confusion of the mind, which creates an endless series of problems and interferes with our clarity of perception so seriously as to prevent us from being able to solve most of them.
>
> . . . Some might say: "Fragmentation of cities, religions, political systems, conflict in the form of wars, general violence, fratricide, etc., are the reality. Wholeness is only an ideal, toward which we should perhaps strive." But this is not what is being said here. Rather, what should be said is that wholeness is what is real, and that fragmentation is the response of this whole to man's action, guided by illusory perception, which is shaped by fragmentary thought. In other words, it is just because reality is whole that man, with his fragmentary approach, will inevitably be answered with a correspondingly fragmentary response. So what is needed is for man to give attention to his habits of fragmentary thought, to be aware of

it, and thus to bring it to an end. Man's approach to reality may then be whole, and so the response will be whole. (1980, 1 and 9)

The roots of perceived fragmentation are extremely deep. Atomic theory, for example, was first proposed by Democritus, who died in 370 B.C.E., and was essentially universalized by Newton in the seventeenth century. It would be difficult to overstate the influence of the Newtonian mind-set, not only on scientific theory and practice but on the whole of Western thought and culture. Its assumptions had a defining influence, for example, on the Industrial Revolution, which in turn became the model for schooling in the twentieth century.

Einstein's theory of relativity challenged many of the premises and conclusions of atomic theory, but quantum theory leveled "a much more serious challenge to this mechanistic order, going far beyond that provided by the theory of relativity" (Bohm, 221). Quantum theory suggests that we live not in an atomized or fragmentary universe, but in a universe of wholeness and interconnection.

"There are no familiar ways to think about the levels of interconnectedness that seem to characterize the quantum universe," Margaret Wheatley notes. "Instead of a lonely void, with isolated particles moving through it, space appears filled with connections. This is why the metaphors turn to webs and weaving, or to the world as a great thought" (1999, 43).

This invisible world of interconnectedness, says Wheatley, is well exemplified by quantum leaps:

Technically, these leaps are abrupt and discontinuous changes, where an electron jumps from one orbit to another without passing through any intermediate stages. It's in one place and then suddenly it's in another, and there are no transition points en route to mark the journey. . . . I know of no better theory to explain the sudden fall of the Berlin Wall, for example. Before the event, there were many small changes going on throughout East Germany, most of which were not visible to anyone beyond their immediate neighborhood. But each small act of defiance or new way of behaving occurred within a whole fabric. Each small act was connected invisibly to all others.

. . . From a Newtonian perspective, our efforts often seem too small, and we doubt our actions will make a difference. Or perhaps we hope that our small efforts will contribute incrementally to large-scale change. Step by step, system by system, we aspire to develop enough mass or force to alter the large system.

But a quantum view explains the success of small efforts quite differently. Acting locally allows us to be inside the movement and flow of the system, participating in all those complex events occurring simultaneously. We are more likely to be sensitive to the dynamics of this system, and thus more effective. However, changes in small places also affect the global system, not through incrementalism, but because every small system participates in an unbroken wholeness. (1999, 44–45)

If all of this seems a bit too theoretical to have bearing on the throbbing necessities of educational leadership, let's bear in mind that the schools and districts we inherited evolved from a factory model, from a Newtonian template. If we try transforming these systems on the basis of Newtonian mental models, we will simply invent new forms of fragmentation. This is evident in standards-based reform efforts, which are revolutionary in conception but have too often been contorted into new forms of fragmentation and factory-like regimentation.

An example of how a standards-based approach is revolutionary in conception is in its movement from a system where time is the constant and the results in student performance, the variable—in other words, teachers move through material at a set pace with some students keeping up and others falling behind or failing—to one where standards are the constant and the time and support needed to achieve them vary according to *individual* student needs (Resnick 1995). But in state after state, as well as through the federal No Child Left Behind Act, standards-based reforms have morphed into high-stakes, standardized test-based accountability systems, where machine-graded tests drive instructional practice into the narrows of test prepping. This factory version of the standards movement ends up recreating systems of sorting and tracking, which are what was supposed to be left behind.

Some critics of public education are too sweeping in their rhetoric when they proclaim that the last several decades of reform have resulted in no progress. But those of us who are committed to the transformation of public education must honestly admit that progress has been painfully slow, and, while studded with striking advances, it has also been riddled with reversals. My argument is that we will not see a quantum leap in education until we are weaned of the perceptual illusion of fragmentation and learn how to see *whole*—the whole system for the whole school for the whole classroom for the whole child.

It is our fragmentary mental models that would have us confining spirituality to the church/temple/mosque compartment of our selves, for those who have such a compartment. But learning to discern what is invisible, we come to a place of greater integration. "The search for meaning, purpose, wholeness and integration is a constant, never-ending task," writes Fred Stokley, who is a retired superintendent. "To confine this search to one day a week or after hours violates people's basic sense of integrity of being whole persons. In short, spirituality is not something one leaves at home" (2002, 50).

What is called for now is spiritual leadership, and the foundation for this new kind of leadership is spiritual consciousness or the capacity to perceive and respond to the hidden wholeness of being. Henry David Thoreau's words of 150 years ago still have the ring of truth: "To be awake is to be alive. . . . We must learn to reawaken and keep ourselves awake, not by mechanical aids, but by an infinite expectation of the dawn, which does not forsake us in our soundest sleep." Spiritually awakened consciousness realizes that the leader's task is not to force a system of schools to be whole, but that its unbroken wholeness can be discovered as an already established, underlying reality. Contemporary author and metapsychiatrist Polly Berrien Berends has come to the same conclusion, though writing on the subject of parenting:

> Like waves on water, leaves on trees, beams from the sun, islands on the earth, everything can be viewed in two ways. Superficially they appear to be separate, isolated, vulnerable, complete things. But looking deeper we find a oneness between each appearance and its underlying source of being: the island is really one with the earth, the leaf with the tree. Every aspect of the whole expresses the whole in unique ways, and the relationship of each to all others is harmoniously governed by the underlying reality with which each is one.
>
> For us then *the quest for wholeness becomes not to acquire, not to accomplish, not to complete our selves—but rather to discover what it is with which we are one so that we can go ahead and be one with it. . . .* Our wholeness already exists and is not something to be given or forced

upon or gotten or taken from each other in the future—but rather, now upon now, awakened to. (1983, 10–11)

From this perspective, the whole system for the whole school for the whole classroom for the whole child is not some ever-beyond-our-reach ideal; it is what underlies the broken surface of misperception. As consciousness awakens to the presence of the whole, political, cultural, and structural obstacles lose some of their obstinance and the possibilities for educational advancement assume new tangibility and traction.

Making and sustaining this shift in consciousness is enormously difficult. We don't gain an inch against the obfuscation of fragmentation by chirping platitudes. As Peter Senge has noted: "We're talking about real, 180-degree change—instead of trying to control everything, we're learning to align our intentions with emerging realities. This is a profound shift in our way of being" (Senge and Wheatley 2002, 65). Yet when educational leaders who are spiritual practitioners and systems thinkers have made this shift, they have found themselves thinking and acting in ways that feel profoundly natural, authentic. They not only feel a fuller connection to reality itself, they discern more of the actual wholeness of the systems they lead and the higher leverage inherent in wholeness.

NOTE

1. The evidence along these lines is enormous. One good example is a study conducted by the Center for Performance Assessment on what they call the "90/90/90 Schools." These are schools with the following characteristics: more than 90 percent of students qualify for a free or reduced price lunch; more than 90 percent of students are ethnic minorities; more than 90 percent of students met or achieved "high academic standards, according to independently conducted tests of academic achievement." The results of this study appear in chapter 19 of D. B. Reeves, *Accountability in Action* (Denver: Advanced Learning Press, 1999).

REFERENCES

Berends, P. B. (1983). *Whole Child/Whole Parent.* New York: Harper & Row.
Bohm, D. (1980). *Wholeness and the Implicate Order.* New York: Routledge Classics.

Fink, S. and S. Thompson (2001). "Standards and Whole System Change." *Teaching and Change* 8, no. 3 (Spring): 237–46.

Fullan, M. (1993). *Change Forces: Probing the Depths of Educational Reform.* Bristol, Pa.: The Falmer Press.

Jaworski, J. (1996). *Synchronicity: The Inner Path of Leadership.* San Francisco: Berrett-Koehler.

———. (1999). "Leadership—Six Essentials." *Perspectives on Business and Global Change* 13, no. 1.

Kahane, A. (2001). "How to Change the World: Lessons from Entrepreneurs from Activists." *Reflections* 2, no. 3: 16–29.

Kim, D. H. (1992). *Systems Archetypes I: Diagnosing Systemic Issues and Designing High-Leverage Interventions.* Waltham, Mass.: Pegasus Communications.

Kohn, A. (2001). "Fighting the Tests: A Practical Guide to Rescuing Our Schools." *Phi Delta Kappan* 82, no. 5 (January): 349–57.

McNeil, L. M. (2000). "Creating New Inequalities: Contradictions of Reform." *Phi Delta Kappan* 81, no. 10 (June): 729–34.

Palmer, P. J. (1993). *To Know As We Are Known: Education as a Spiritual Journey.* San Francisco: HarperSanFrancisco.

Resnick, L. (1995). "From Aptitude to Effort: A New Foundation for Our Schools." *Daedalus* 124, no. 4 (Fall): 55–62.

Scharmer, C. O. (2000). "Presencing: Learning from the Future As It Emerges." Paper presented at the Conference on Knowledge and Innovation, May 25–26, Helsinki School of Economics, Finland, 1–64.

Schemo, D. J., and F. Fessenden (2003). "Gains in Houston Schools: How Real Are They?" *New York Times,* December 3, A1 and A24.

Senge, P. M. (1990). *The Fifth Discipline: The Art and Practice of the Learning Organization.* New York: Currency Doubleday.

Senge, P. M. and M. Wheatley (2002). "Changing How We Work Together." *Reflections* 3, no. 3 (Spring): 63–67; reprinted from *The Shambhala Sun* (2001).

Senge, P. M., et al. (1994). *The Fifth Discipline Fieldbook: Strategies and Tools for Building a Learning Organization.* New York: Currency Doubleday.

Stokley, F. (2002). "What It Means to Be a Spiritual Leader." *The School Administrator* 8, no. 59 (September): 48–50.

Thompson, S. (1999). "Systems Thinking: Untangling the Gordian Knots of Systemic Change." *Strategies* 6, no. 1 (July): 1–3.

———. (2001). "The Authentic Standards Movement and Its Evil Twin." *Phi Delta Kappan* 82, no. 5 (January): 358–62.

———. (2003a). "A High-Performance School System." In F. M. Duffy, *Courage, Passion, and Vision: A Guide to Leading Systemic School Improvement*, 101–12. Lanham, Md.: Scarecrow Press.

———. (2003b). "Children Get Left Behind When High Stakes Are Confused with High Leverage." *Nochildleft.Com* 1, no. 3 (March).

Wheatley, M. J. (1999). *Leadership and the New Science: Discovering Order in a Chaotic World.* 2d ed. San Francisco: Berrett-Koehler.

CHAPTER 3

Called to Serve

> The superintendency isn't so much a job as it is a calling. You may choose it, but it also chooses you. You are summoned to it.
>
> —Paul Houston (2001)

It's an intuitive experience that many people have had—the sense of being called to a particular opportunity, community, or field of endeavor. It is often simply a recognition that "this is what I'm supposed to do" or "where I'm supposed to be right now."

A sense of calling is especially common to educators. It's not a profession, like law or medicine, promising plump salaries or professional prestige. It is perhaps more akin to missionary or social work, where working with and for a sense of purpose is the principal reward.

In his book *To Teach: The Journey of a Teacher*, William Ayers describes the sense of calling that has drawn so many educators into their profession:

> People are called to teaching because they love children and youth, or because they love being with them, watching them open up and grow and become able, more competent, more powerful in the world. They may love what happens to themselves when they are with children, the ways in which they become their best selves. Or they become teachers because they love the world or some piece of the world enough that they want to show that love to others. In either case, people teach as an act of construction and as a gift of oneself to others. (1993, 8)

Ayers's final observation in this passage is an important one. Teaching is "a gift of oneself to others." When people are called to teach, they are called to serve—to serve a purpose that is larger than one's self-interest, to serve their students' need for education, and to serve parents' and the community's need to have their children be educated. The root of *educate, educere*, means "to lead forth." Educators are called to the sacred work of leading forth our children, unfolding the potential that lies within each child. In Danish, the word for *education* means "show the wonder."

Being called is a spiritual experience, because both the call and what we are called to do connect us to a purpose or source beyond the limits of the ego-self. "The notion of vocation comes from spiritual and philosophical traditions," writes Margaret Wheatley. "It describes work that is given to us, that we are meant to do. We don't decide what our vocation is. We receive it. It always originates from outside us. Therefore, we can't talk about vocation or calling without acknowledging that there is something going on beyond our narrow sense of self. It helps remind us that there's more than just me, that we're part of a larger and purpose-filled place" (2002, 42).

While Ayers's observations on the call to teach were made in 1993, a more recent study from Public Agenda reaches similar conclusions on the basis of extensive surveys, complemented by several focus groups, with new teachers (five or fewer years of experience), principals, and superintendents: "New teachers are quick to point out that theirs is a profession that requires a sense of mission. More than 8 in 10 (86%) believe only those with 'a true sense of calling' should pursue the work" (Farkas, Johnson, and Foleno 2000, 10).

Although the Public Agenda study found that only 12 percent of new teachers surveyed say they fell into a career in education by chance (11), I found more of a mix in my interviews for this book between those who had a definite sense of calling and those who more or less stumbled into education. But what seems significant to me is that even those who wound up in education by happenstance developed a deep commitment and sense of mission in their work as educators and educational leaders. For example, LaVaun Dennett, who started out as a teacher and went on to become the principal of several schools and is currently a central office director, says she got into education "by accident." But she adds that "a lot of times the more important things that have happened to me came about unexpectedly. I just love the work and happen to feel that it is the most important work on the planet. There's nothing like watching someone—student or adult—struggle with a concept and then get it."

For some who have felt called into education, it wasn't simply a flash of recognition, but a whole set of life circumstances that shaped the imperative to be an educator. Betty Jo Webb, for example, grew up in an impoverished African American community in rural Louisiana. She explains that there were two major positions in a segregated black community in that time and place: teacher and preacher.

> Everybody looked up to those folks. I was inspired to want to get out of the condition [of extreme poverty] very early. And it was instilled in us very early that the way out is to get a good education. We had as role models people that dedicated their lives to teaching us. I carried that admiration for teachers all the way through. I always wanted to go to college and become a teacher. I would call it a calling. It still is. No matter how I've tried to walk away from education (and I did try some other things) I finally realized that there's no dodging this work—that this is a calling for me. And while I may not always do it in the same position or the same way, I will always be connected to education.

SERVING, LEADING

Virtually no educational leaders started out as educational leaders. Most began as teachers. A few came from other fields. Most were not so much called to lead—at least not initially—as they were called to teach and thus called to serve. What is critically important when making the transition into a position of formal leadership is to stay in touch with the original call, to realize that a commitment to service is not something you can leave behind as you ascend the organizational hierarchy. (Of course, becoming an educational leader does not always involve moving up the ladder, as any teacher leader would be quick to point out.)

Les Omotani, who recently resigned as superintendent of West Des Moines Community Schools in Iowa to accept a superintendency on Long Island, has spent his entire career in education. He believes that service is at the heart of educational leadership: "What I put on the lead cover of my resume application from my first position to the one I used when I joined West Des Moines Community Schools in 1995 is that simple phrase, 'To serve them all my days.' So I have stuck with that for a long time. I really do believe that the leadership function is one of both service and leadership."

It was Robert Greenleaf who coined the phrase and developed the concept of *servant-leadership* with the publication in 1970 of an essay called *The Servant as Leader,* where he says that servant-leadership "begins with the natural feeling that one wants to serve, to serve first. Then conscious choice brings one to aspire to lead. The difference manifests itself in the care taken by the servant—first to make sure that other people's highest-priority needs are being served. The best test is: Do those served grow as persons; do they, while being served, become healthier, wiser, freer, more autonomous, more likely themselves to become servants?" (quoted in Spears, 4).

This idea certainly emerged from Greenleaf's own half-century of experience in the corporate world, but what directly triggered the paradoxical image of servant-leader was his response to reading a work of fiction by Hermann Hesse called *Journey to the East*. Greenleaf summarizes the story:

> In this story we see a band of men on a mythical journey. . . . The central figure of the story is Leo, who accompanies the party as the servant who does the menial chores, but who also sustains them with his spirit and his song. He is a person of extraordinary presence. All goes well until Leo disappears. Then the group falls into disarray and the journey is abandoned. They cannot make it without the servant Leo. The narrator, one of the party, after some years of wandering, finds Leo and is taken into the Order that had sponsored the journey. There he discovers that Leo, whom he had known first as servant, was in fact the titular head of the Order, its guiding spirit, a great and noble *leader*. (Quoted in Sergiovanni 1992, 124)

The leader as servant makes a striking appearance in Christian scriptures, in the thirteenth chapter of John's gospel, as well. Immediately following his last supper with his disciples before the crucifixion, Jesus poured water into a basin and washed their feet. The account concludes: "After washing their feet and taking his garments again, he sat down. 'Do you understand what I have done for you?' he asked. 'You call me "Master" and "Lord," and rightly so, for that is what I am. Then if I, your Lord and Master, have washed your feet, you also ought to wash one another's feet. I have set you an example: you are to do as I have done for you.'"

The concept of leadership has sometimes evoked images of a charismatic or autocratic figure, lording it over his or her followers, compelling them into compliance. Greenleaf, Hesse, and the recorded words and actions of Jesus all challenge this conception of leadership. They consciously blur the distinction between leadership and service.

This sense of service, at the heart of authentic leadership, is not only service to others, service to followers, but also service to a greater purpose, and service to followers by helping them discover and be committed to the same greater purpose. Servant-leaders recognize that trusting and open relationships are indispensable to organizational development, and so they work hard to remove cultural and structural barriers to trust and openness and endeavor to model trustworthiness and openness in their actions as leaders. According to Dennett, servant-leadership is about "really trying to listen to people, to their hearts and their dreams that are sometimes hidden behind things. You're constantly taking away barriers."

Servant-leaders also recognize that people are far more likely to invest in or be committed to endeavors or organizations where they have developed a sense of joint ownership. For this and other reasons, servant-leaders tend to actively and broadly engage stakeholders in decisions and processes that elicit their ownership and that tap into diverse perspectives and perceptions. (Building trust, openness, and ownership is the subject of chapter 5.)

As director of curriculum, instruction, and assessment in Norwalk–La Mirada Unified School District, Dennett supervises a diverse staff with multiple responsibilities. "I can build on a common goal that we have but use the expertise *they* have to do something far, far better than I would ever be able to do on my own," Dennett explains. "If they didn't take initiative to go ahead and do it, we wouldn't get nearly as good a product. It's like this dance that we do where sometimes they lead me, and sometimes I lead them."

Servant-leaders also invest the time and energy needed to develop shared vision and to discover and communicate organization-wide core values, and in the process they stir passions and solidify commitment to the essential work of serving all students by helping them realize more and more of their intellectual and personal potential. Servant-leaders are impelled in their work by moral purpose, passion, and courage. (The vision and values aspect of servant-leadership is explored in depth in chapter 6. Chapter 8 is a reflection on moral purpose, moral passion, and moral courage in educational leadership.)

"Servant-leadership is not about a personal quest for power, prestige, or material rewards," Ann McGee-Cooper and Duane Trammell point out (1999). And one could argue that this makes it a particularly apt fit for educational leadership, which offers comparatively little in the way of power, prestige, or material rewards! "The focus of servant-leadership is on sharing information, building common vision, self-management, high levels of interdependence, learning from mistakes, encouraging creative input from every team member, and questioning present assumptions and mental models."

Serving the needs of an organization by serving the needs of its people does not necessarily mean always being congenial or passive. "You're a servant to a larger end and a servant to those charged with getting there," says Stephen Fink, who was an assistant superintendent in the Edmonds School District outside of Seattle and is now the director of the Center for Educational Leadership at the University of Washington. "To be a servant-leader is to be a critical friend. A critical friend is more than a friend, and a servant-leader is more than a servant. It involves having the moral compass, and therefore the fortitude and the courage and the spirit of service to tell someone that they are not doing what they need to do to be an effective, competent, morally anchored leader. If I don't do that then I'm not really serving you as a deep, spiritual being."

On the other hand, what gets communicated and how it gets communicated matter greatly. A leader's success in serving the organization by serving its purpose and supporting its people depends upon his or her ability to convey a spirit of support and mutual ownership even when confronting shortcomings. Timothy Lucas, who was an assistant superintendent in the Glen Rock School District in New Jersey when I interviewed him (and is now teaching educational leadership at Lehigh University), speaks of his evolution as a servant-leader:

In my own experiences as a school leader I can remember times when a teacher came to me with an idea and I would say "that will never work." And I pretty much shut down any energy that person had to be creative. It took me four or five months, and this person said, "Well, I came to you with an idea, and you just shot it down. So why would I come to you with any other ideas?" And then I started to realize that it's that daily interaction with people that creates a much bigger atmosphere. And when you look at the servant-leadership piece, that's what it's really about. My job is to sit here and truly listen and take in and let it move through me who this person is, instead of reacting to words. There's a feedback that goes on at a different level. It's about relationships. It's hard to measure. There are days when I don't know what I've accomplished in terms of facilitating groups, moving them along, and guiding them more or less. But over time you start to see the feedback.

When I visualize it, servant-leadership means that I'm not in the center. It puts me somewhere in the system, facilitating the system.

One key emphasis in servant-leadership is building purposeful relationships, where followers feel supported even as they are challenged to move beyond the current reality of their performance. Another key emphasis is allowing time and space for individual and collective reflection. And this takes considerable courage in the face of political pressure to get test scores up (Wheatley 1999).

We've already mentioned three additional chapters in this book that explore facets of servant-leadership. In fact, much of the remainder of this book comprises chapters that chart the dimensions of servant-leadership, which, if not a synonym, is certainly a close sibling of spiritual leadership. For example, "Humility in High Places" (chapter 11) delves into a distinguishing attribute of servant-leaders: the humility that enables them to devote their energies to building up not their own egos or careers, but the organizations or systems they serve as leaders, as well as the people who give the organization or system its identity and capacity. "What Power Had I Before I Learned to Yield?" (chapter 10) also expands on a defining element of servant-leadership: the dispersion of leadership authority across the system as the means of unleashing creative potential.

"Leading is giving. It is serving," according to Fred Stokley, retired superintendent of Ridgewood Village School District in New Jersey.

"Leadership is an ethic—a gift of oneself to a common cause, a higher calling. . . . When their gifts are genuine and the spirit is right, their giving transforms a school or school district from a mere place of work to a shared way of life" (2002, 50).

REFERENCES

Ayers, W. (1993). *To Teach: The Journey of a Teacher*. New York: Teachers College Press.

Farkas, S., J. Johnson, and T. Foleno (2000). *A Sense of Calling: Who Teaches and Why.* New York: Public Agenda.

Houston, P. (2001). "Superintendents for the 21st Century: It's Not Just a Job, It's a Calling." *Phi Delta Kappan* 82, no. 6 (February).

McGee-Cooper, A., and D. Trammell (1999). "From Hero As Leader to Servant As Leader." *The Systems Thinker* 10, no. 3. www.pegasuscom.com/levpoints/servlead.html.

Sergiovanni, T. J. (1992). *Moral Leadership: Getting to the Heart of School Improvement*. San Francisco: Jossey-Bass.

Spears, L. C., ed. (1995). *Reflections on Leadership: How Robert K. Greenleaf's Theory of Servant-Leadership Influenced Today's Top Management Thinkers*. New York: John Wiley and Sons.

Stokely, F. (2002). "What It Means to Be a Spiritual Leader." *The School Administrator* 59, no. 8 (September): 48–50.

Wheatley, M. J. (1999, June). "Servant-leadership and Community Leadership in the 21st Century." Keynote address, The Robert K. Greenleaf Center for Servant Leadership annual conference. www.margaretwheatley.com/articles/servantleader.html.

———. (2002). "Spirituality in Turbulent Times." *The School Administrator* 8, no. 59 (September): 42–46.

CHAPTER 4

Habits of Spiritual Leaders

Hold fast the time! Guard it, watch over it, every hour, every minute! Unguarded it slips away like a lizard, smooth, slippery, faithless. Hold every moment sacred. Give each clarity and meaning, each the weight of thine awareness, each its true and due fulfillment.

—Thomas Mann

If humanity is to be fulfilled, rather than enslaved by continuous acquiescence in finitude, we desperately need reminders of who we are. We need whatever articulates the core "humanness" of which we must become sharply conscious in order to make choices that do not oppress.

—Allison W. Phinney

We live in a world where change is not only constant, but is constantly accelerating. Technological advances have the paradoxical effect of adding to the pace and complexity of our lives by virtue of the very ease, comfort, and velocity they afford.

For educational leaders, rapid action is the fabric of the workday. The intensity and complexity of this work explain, in part, the famously brief average tenure of an urban superintendent.

The spiritual dimensions of educational leadership are scarcely discernible, much less nourished, in the social upheaval and political turmoil that fundamental reform arouses. In such an environment, a spiritual perspective can only be gained through considerable discipline. As educational consultant John Morefield observes:

> Leadership is really hard. And educational leadership is only getting harder. You sure as hell don't do it for fame and fortune. The only reason I can see that people stick with it over time is because they have some sense of calling to do leadership work on behalf of children, and it comes from some deep well within them.
>
> I do a lot of work with folks on "How do you sustain this? How do you keep the fire lit? How do you avoid putting too many logs on the fire and making the fire smoulder? How do you keep the spaces in between the logs so that flames can live? What are those spaces? What are the spaces for you? Do you have any? Do you fill your life up, leaving no space?" The sustaining of one's well-being, one's health, is important; it allows deeply committed people to stay for the long haul.[1]

Morefield points out that the development of this kind of spiritual sustenance requires "sacred spaces," which must intentionally be created and preserved. "We have to take action to create inaction. . . . That inaction is not passive in the sense that there is work happening."

Spiritual leadership is not possible without a cultivated and disciplined commitment to seeking out what is hidden beneath surface appearances. Nothing in the political context of educational leadership supports such discipline. It must be discovered and nurtured from within, and a spiritual leader must vigilantly guard against the river of externals that is constantly ready to sweep it away.

Educational reformers have sometimes spoken and written about the "noise" that tends to surround change efforts—a mental and emotional commotion that makes it difficult to stay focused on the core of the endeavor. What has rarely been mentioned in relation to educational practice and reform, however, is the place and importance of "silence." Silence is commonly understood to be the absence of noise, but Gerald Schiffhorst has written about a kind of silence that is not absence but "a positive force in itself. . . . It is not about emptiness or negativity but about presence"(1999, 44).

This silence that is presence is a powerful counterweight to the systemic noise that tends to stall educational progress by pulling everyone's attention off focus. While the heart of the work is children's learning, the noise is mostly about the dynamics of adult concerns and the playing out of old scripts. A leader who has cultivated spiritual silence is better able to help others to keep the real work in focus. He or she is spiritually grounded, and that grounding is a source of authenticity and authority. It is less evidenced by words than by a stability and clarity in the face of shifting or conflicting political crosscurrents.

"THE AWAKENING HOUR"

"The morning, which is the most memorable season of the day, is the awakening hour," Thoreau observes in *Walden*. "Then there is least somnolence in us; and for an hour, at least, some part of us awakes which slumbers all the rest of the day and night."

An educational leader's workday is bound to be crowded with events, cluttered with preoccupations, and riddled with requirements. The leader might steal a moment during the workday, here or there, for reading or reflecting, but a meaningful spiritual perspective is not likely to be snatched on the fly. Many spiritual practitioners have found the quiet of early morning to be an indispensable sanctuary for gaining spiritual ground. Consider, for example, the words of Dietrich Bonhoeffer, the legendary Lutheran pastor, who died at the hands of Nazis for his courageous participation in the German underground:

> Each morning is a new beginning of our life. Each day is a finished whole. . . . Every morning God gives us the gift of comprehending anew his faithfulness of old; thus, in the midst of our life with God, we may daily begin a new life with him. . . . The first moments of the new day are not the time for our own plans and worries, not even for our zeal to accomplish our own work, but for God's liberating grace, God's sanctifying presence. (1986, 31, 32)

John Kammerud, who is superintendent of Mauston School District in Wisconsin, has developed the habit of listening to reflective music in his office for about fifteen minutes at the start of each day. He reads the Bible or poetry before strenuous meetings in order to gain the sense of stillness and spiritual grounding the situation calls for.

The sources of spiritual nourishment and renewal, of course, can be highly individualistic. For many it will involve some form of communion with their God; for others it might involve ritualistic practices, prayer, or meditating on images that are significant for them; for yet others it might involve walking in the woods, writing in a journal, or getting reconnected to the passionate core of their values and beliefs. All of these have the potential of being disciplines, if developed and honed through habitual and mindful practice. Early morning is not the only time for the exercise of spiritual habits, but for working professionals—especially if they have family or community obligations in the evenings—it is often the one time of day that is most easily protected and most naturally ripe.

In the words of the Hebrew poet David:

> In the morning thou wilt hear my voice;
> In the morning I will lay it before thee and wait.
> —Psalms 5:3

TIME

Anyone who has been an educator or has worked closely with educators knows that somewhere very close to the top of virtually every educator's list of factors that stand in the way of progress is time constraints. This is true for teachers and for educational leaders at all levels. Everything that meaningful educational practice and reform demands takes time, whether it's developing collaborative relationships, engaging in professional development, writing and refining content and performance standards, developing new curricula or assessments, intervening in a low-performing school, or any of myriad other tasks. But it's not as though the ongoing demands that have already been consuming educators' every spare moment can be magically suspended.

Similarly, the discipline of spiritual leadership requires some of that essential, scarce resource: time. "Making time to quiet myself and travel inwards is difficult at times," says Mark Bielang, who is superintendent of public schools in Paw Paw, Michigan. "I find I have to schedule those moments of reflection." And because the substance and influence of spirituality is hidden, it's especially hard to make time for spiritual practice. But there's an important paradox in spiritual practice that educational leaders neglect to their own detriment: While spiritual practice takes time, it also can have a liberating effect in relation to the imprisoning experience of time. Spiritual practitioners have often found that their discipline sets them free.

Here's an example from my own experience of gaining some measure of dominion over the tyranny of time by making time for spiritual practice. For most of my life since my early teens, I have taken time each morning for prayer and spiritual study. For me, this gives grounding to my whole day. It helps me be more open to what is spiritually possible and more ready to meet challenges from a position of inner strength.

I spent the fall term of my senior year in college on a study program in Great Britain. The academic work included three courses: a comprehensive study of English literature (from Bede up to the brink of the twentieth century), the history of England, and an independent creative writing seminar. We were expected to do most of the reading during the summer prior to this trip. As it turned out, I had a demanding job at an international daily newspaper that summer and only got about halfway through the reading list. During our travels through England, Scotland, and Wales, there was much to see and experience and only so much time for reading. And so there came a day near the end of the trip when I had to hand in a short essay on each of the literary pieces we were supposed to have read and a longer essay on Winston Churchill's four-volume history of the English-speaking people. While I had made some progress along the way, I still had a considerable amount of reading to do and four short essays and one longer paper to write.

On the day before the papers were due, as you can imagine, I was sorely tempted to skip my spiritual work and plunge into the academic work that needed doing. The temptation sounded something like this: "You know, it's not sensible to spend time in spiritual study now. That won't get you ahead on all this work. If you've got any sense, you'll do the work and worry about praying and that kind of stuff later."

But the voice didn't feel trustworthy, and as I thought about it, it occurred to me that what I needed more than time was to be in closer touch with the very source of life and consciousness and possibility. And so I took time that morning not just to glance over some familiar passages in the Bible, but to study and listen and pray as I read.

Although I didn't see much of London on that particular day, I had a wonderful time doing the work that needed to be done. In the past I had always handwritten papers and then typed the final draft on the typewriter. (This was shortly before the advent of the PC. In those days if you made a typing error it often involved retyping the page or, in some cases, typing the whole document again from scratch.) That day I found myself rolling the paper into the typewriter and watching the words tumble out into first-effort final drafts. The words flowed with a vibrancy that seemed as natural as having a good conversation. The day was not draining, but stimulating and inspiring. I worked hard, but was unpressured and found I could take time to have afternoon tea with the English family I was staying with. And based on my professor's extremely positive reaction to the papers, it seems safe to conclude that I wasn't simply kidding myself into believing that they were better than they actually were.

This experience, and other similar experiences that I've had since then, caused me to reconsider the nature of time constraints. Perhaps it is not time that we so desperately need. Consider two people who are nearly identical in knowledge and talent and who are assigned the task of writing a substantial grant proposal to a foundation. Person A comes to the task with a spirit of inspiration, expectation, and intellectual and creative vitality, while person B comes to it with a sense of stress and writer's block. Person B could be given four times the amount of time for the assignment and still come up short of the quality of the proposal that person A writes. The same would hold for the development of an accountability system or professional development plan. Even when it comes to filling out bureaucratic forms in triplicate, one's state of mind can still trump time constraints.

I don't exactly mean to imply that taking time for spiritual practice makes time for other things. It's more that taking time for spiritual practice brings out more of what is otherwise hidden: more inspiration, more wisdom, more creative energy, more grounding, and a greater ability to move or flow with what is naturally unfolding.

SACRIFICE

When a virtuoso musician or athlete takes our breath away by making an astonishing accomplishment look nearly effortless, we are seeing not just exceptional talent but the fruits of sacrifice. The countless hours of practice that made the performance possible came, of course, at a steep cost. More often than not, such individuals were willing to make the sacrifice because their love of the art or sport was greater than their love of what they were giving up in all those hours of practice.

And such sacrifice often extends beyond the individual to close family members, friends, and supporters. In fact, any devoted parent quickly becomes completely familiar with the taste of sacrifice.

Spirituality that is substantial and meaningful—spirituality that is something more than the occasional feel-good bromide—is born of sacrifice, is the fruit of persistent practice.

PERSISTENCE

Consistency of practice is essential if one's spirituality is to be meaningfully experienced and developed. In this sense, spiritual practices need to become habitual. At the same time, one must stay alert that habitual practices not become unthinking routines in which the practitioner is simply jumping through a hoop of a different shape. What is called for in spiritual practice is persistently renewed mindfulness.

Here we are talking about persistence in two different, but ultimately interdependent, ways.

1. Each spiritual endeavor requires the spiritual practitioner's persistence. When we sit to pray, study, reflect, or meditate, we will at times feel spiritually disconnected, distracted, or apathetic. As there is resistance to change in education, so there is internal resistance to spiritual growth and renewal. If we always wait for a better, more inspired, time for our spiritual practice, we will likely find that our procrastination has become a staunch ally with that which resists our spiritual development. So don't delay, persist.

> Be dogged in seeking to reconnect with the source of purpose, meaning, inspiration, and spiritual grounding.

2. We will also need to be persistent over time in terms of regular practice across months, years, and decades. It's that long-term persistence that opens our lives to experiential dimensions that would otherwise remain concealed under materialism's bright and distracting surfaces.

As Annie Dillard notes: "There is no shortage of good days. It is good lives that are hard to come by. A life of good days in the senses is not enough. The life of sensation is the life of greed; it requires more and more. The life of the spirit requires less and less; time is ample and its passage sweet" (1989, 32–33).

This subject brings to mind a story that LaVaun Dennett, who was a principal and educational consultant before becoming a district-level director in Norwalk–La Mirada Unified School District near Los Angeles, tells:

> There's a story about a donkey who fell in a well. The farmer comes over and looks down the well and says "This is an old donkey; the well is very deep, and I'm never going to be able to get him out of there. By the time I figured out how to get this rope around his neck, I'd kill him bringing him up. I'm just going to bury him in the well."
>
> He throws a shovelful of dirt. The donkey shakes it off his back and dances around. The farmer keeps throwing in dirt, and the donkey keeps shaking it off and stomping it down. The next thing you know, he is standing on top, because the farmer filled the well and the donkey walks out.
>
> No matter how much dirt somebody throws in there or that we throw on our selves, you can keep shaking it off and say, "OK, I can stand on this and go some place." People don't believe in themselves, and when you help them believe in themselves they do things that surprise everybody.

Perseverance is one of the distinguishing qualities of outstanding leaders. It becomes its own blessing, for as Dillard has also observed, "Nothing on earth is more gladdening than knowing we must roll up our sleeves and move back the boundaries of the humanly possible once more" (1989, 98).

COMPASSION

Spirituality is replete with paradoxes, including one mentioned above: taking time for the exercise of spiritual discipline alleviates, rather than exacerbates, time constraints. Here's another: The inner work of spiritual practice is not self-absorbing, but leads one's thought and heart upward and outward.

Compassion is an important measure of spiritual authenticity, and it's essential to spiritual leadership for whole-system transformation in education. Why? Because full-scale change is disruptive, painful, and too complex not to be loaded with false starts and missteps. All of this is true not just for leaders but for stakeholders throughout the system. When the status quo gets disrupted and routines are shaken, people find themselves at an uncomfortable and risky distance from the familiar. Leaders who ignore this suffering undercut the foundational trust, openness, and ownership on which cultural and structural transformations must be built (see next chapter). But a compassionate leader recognizes what fellow stakeholders are going through and communicates verbally and practically rock-solid support.

"I think that religion is filled with examples of mercy," says Carol Johnson, who was superintendent of Minneapolis Public Schools when I interviewed her and has since taken on the superintendency in Memphis. "One of the things that educational leaders can bring to their work is trying to operationalize that spiritual mercy in concrete ways. It's this ability to understand that part of being spiritually connected is understanding your imperfections well enough to be merciful and patient with those who are imperfect. There have been times when my spiritual faith was the only thing that allowed me to forgive."

Such compassion needs to extend not only outward, but also inward, and this too is essential. Educational leaders would do well to heed the advice of Ralph Waldo Emerson: "Finish every day and be done with it. You have done what you could. Some blunders and absurdities no doubt crept in; forget them as soon as you can. Tomorrow is a new day; begin it well and serenely and with too high a spirit to be encumbered with your nonsense."

NOTE

1. John Morefield explained to me that he drew the metaphor of the fire from a poem called "Fire" in *The Sea Accepts All Rivers and Other Poems*, by Judy Sorum Brown (Alexandria, Va.. Miles River Press, 2000).

REFERENCES

Bielang, M. T. (2003). Standing Still in the Wilderness. *The School Administrator* 60(8): 36.

Bonhoeffer, D. (1986). *Meditating on the Word*. Trans. D. McI. Gracie. New York: Ballantine Books.

Dillard, A. (1989). *The Writing Life*. New York: HarperPerennial.

Schiffhorst, G. (1999). "Etty Hillesum and the Language of Silence." *Mars Hill Review* 14 (summer): 43–50.

CHAPTER 5

Groundwork: Trust, Openness, and Ownership

Have you ever noticed that before a new building goes up there is month upon month of what looks like a lot of digging around in the dirt? And then haven't you been astonished to see how rapidly the structure is erected once the foundation has been laid? The messy, protracted groundwork is indispensable for a new and durable structure (Thompson, 1995).

It's a lesson that has been too often overlooked by educational leaders and reformers. A chief reason for this is that while buildings have literal foundations in the ground, the foundations of sustainable systemic reforms in public education are quite a bit more subtle and complex. Even so, the digging is essential. Here's the key question: What is underneath a systemic reform effort that is indispensable to its sustainability?

I would argue that the foundation for sustainable educational improvement involves three closely related essentials: trust, openness, and shared ownership. The groundwork also involves the development of shared vision and identification of core values, but vision and values are the subject of the next chapter.

TRUST

Consider another metaphor. Traction matters. Take the highest-powered sports car you can think of, get it into a situation where the tires have no traction, and then you can ride the accelerator and gun the engine so that the tires are furiously spinning, but the vehicle will make no forward progress. Keep it up and you'll drain the fuel tank and really be in a pickle. But the moment you give the tires some traction, the situation changes dramatically.

Trust gives traction to large-scale reforms. Or, as Robert Evans puts it, "Transformation begins with trust" (1996, 183). The problem with the spinning tire is that it isn't connecting with solid ground. For large-scale improvement to take hold, connections are essential, and these connections are made out of trust.

The importance of trust can be seen in a single school. Whether that school is engaged in substantial reform or not, "an interrelated set of mutual dependencies are embedded within [its] social exchanges" (Bryk and Schneider 2003, 41). While an effective principal may be indispensable to a strong school, that principal nevertheless relies on his or her staff daily to exercise ethical and professional judgments and to participate as members of an educational community. Teachers, in turn, are not only dependent upon the principal for the leadership and management of their school, but also upon the professionalism of their teaching colleagues. Parents of course depend on the school staff as a whole to keep their children safe and learning. "Such dependencies create a sense of mutual vulnerability for all individuals involved," Bryk and Schneider observe. "Consequently, deliberate action taken by any party to reduce this sense of vulnerability in others—to make them feel safe and secure—builds trust across the community" (41).

Bryk and Schneider compared extensive survey responses in high- and low-performing Chicago public schools on three measures of relational trust: teacher-principal, teacher-teacher, and teacher-parent. They also note that the survey results are consistent with field observations made over a period of years in Chicago schools. Their research reveals that top quartile schools are characterized by high levels of trust between teachers. In these schools, about three-quarters of teachers say they have "strong" or "very strong" trust relations with fellow teachers. Schools in the bottom quartile, however, tell an altogether different tale. Most teachers in these schools report low trust and respect among teachers (Bryk and Schneider 2002, 94; see also Payne and Kaba 2001).

Bryk and Schneider found similar results with respect to the level of trust between teachers and principals, with nearly all teachers in top quartile schools feeling very good about their relationship with their principal and teachers in bottom quartile schools generally indicating a perceived lack of respect from their principal (95).

It cuts both ways. In the absence of trust, new ideas and possibilities for improvement get minimized or even closed out. But where trust is present, there's an openness that allows for connections with new ideas, approaches, or possibilities, as well as connections with colleagues and a corresponding willingness to form collaborative relationships. And most importantly, these conditions have considerable influence on the quality of teaching and learning.

"One way we build trust is we agree to do something we think is important," author Carl Glickman points out. "The first resistance on the road is a testing of commitment and trust to what we agreed on. If we cave in, because one person can make life miserable for us, without working through the issue, trust becomes a casualty. Can we trust that we really are going to move ahead with what we believe? That doesn't mean being congenial, sometimes it means really being pretty frank."

If a paucity of trust can hamper or even paralyze the progress of individual schools, it can clearly be a destructive force when magnified and projected across a larger system. The devastating effects of distrust and the critical role of the restoration of trust in leading systemic improvement are both well illustrated by Sacramento City Unified School District.

In the mid-1990s the system was in chaos. Not only was student performance lagging—with nearly half of 52,000 students performing in the bottom third in the nation, according to SAT-9 reading and math scores—but buildings were in disrepair, the morale of teachers and administrators was sagging, and relations between the district administration, the school board, and the teachers union were acrimonious (Cohen 2002).[1]

In 1995, Mayor Joe Serna commissioned a report that documented the depth and extent of the problems the school system faced. When the school board dismissed the report, Serna organized a slate of four candidates in the next election of the seven-member school board. The slate won, and in February of 1997 the new board promoted deputy superintendent Jim Sweeney to interim superintendent and made him the official superintendent that October.

In time, Sweeney and his leadership team created and implemented a multifaceted action plan that has resulted in significant improvement in student performance levels and a narrowing of the gap between poor and minority students and their more advantaged peers. But none of this could have been accomplished if Sweeney had not attended to the crucial groundwork.

To begin the work of restoring a climate of trust within schools and repairing the badly damaged relationship between schools and central office, Sweeney began holding weekly meetings, dubbed "fireside chats," in schools. The meetings were open to all comers, and Sweeney says that his role was primarily to listen and respond, not to present or hold forth. Several school board members were usually present at these meetings as well. "We did a lot of grassroots stuff, just talking with people," Sweeney says. "You just wear away all that cynicism."

Later, when a newly designed accountability system and strategic plan were created, Sweeney spent three months in schools explaining their purpose and gathering feedback. "After everyone had a chance to review the plan, Sweeney convened a meeting in March 1998 of more than 4,500 employees at the ARCO sports arena, where the overwhelming majority of participants signed a pledge and received a 'count me in' button" (Cohen).

It needs to be emphasized that a host of important factors—clarity of vision and strategic direction, heavy investments in curriculum redesign and intensive, high-quality professional development, extensive and skillful use of data for accountability and continuous improvement, and many others—contributed to the noteworthy systemic progress that has been achieved in Sacramento. It is also fair to say that the foundation for systemic improvement in Sacramento was the restoration of a climate of trust and openness. Reculturing prepared the soil for significant restructuring.

Trust and Race

In a nation with a long history of race-based disparities and injustices, it comes as no surprise that race can be a huge barrier to the development of trust in classrooms, schools, and school systems. "For me as a white person who has chosen to be a white ally [to people of color] in the struggle for social justice, I never assumed a person of color would automatically trust me," says John Morefield, who for twenty years was a principal in Seattle schools, where children of color outnumber white children.

During one of his principalships, Morefield had an hour-long encounter with the outraged grandfather of an African-American boy who was a student in the school. Morefield believes that in many schools the boy would probably have been labeled ADHD, "but we were really trying to see if we could not have him medicated." Morefield was working closely and well with the boy's mother, trying to address his needs. As part of the plan they worked out, the boy could sometimes attend the school for part of the day and spend the rest of the school day in an alternative placement.

Morefield explained that the boy's grandfather got extremely upset about having the boy in alternative placement. After several angry phone calls, the grandfather set up an appointment with Morefield.

> It was one of those appointments from hell, where I just sat there and listened to him and his anger and rage about what was happening to his grandson. And it appeared that there was more than that that was coming out, and I was the person who was receiving the brunt of it. I do remember at that time going through all the emotions of defensiveness and anger and fear and all of that and hearing pretty ugly accusations on my character. I had to consciously choose to go to a different place. I consciously and silently used the "self talk": "Well, this is not about my competence or my motives. I do know that I'm open to the fact that maybe the actions we are taking were not *necessarily* the right ones. But these names he's calling me don't define me." It moved me into a place that allowed me to hear. And then at the end, when he for the most part was spent, I calmly and firmly stated what we were trying to do again and asked for him to work with us in finding alternatives. At that point, he said "I'll get back to you." Then he came back the next day, and we were able to have a two-way conversation.

Morefield's experience says a great deal about what trust-building requires of a leader, especially when suspicion and anger have racial roots. His considerable self-knowledge and compassion enabled him to be a persevering listener instead of reacting argumentatively. When the grandfather had thoroughly vented his anger, fears, and accusations, Morefield reaffirmed his desire to work together in seeking an effective alternative for the man's grandson.

Deborah Meier, principal of Mission Hill School in Boston, describes in her book *In Schools We Trust* the struggles she and her colleagues had confronting racial barriers to the trust that is so essential to educational progress. "Exploring rage and guilt over white privilege is one approach for bringing difficult issues up front," she writes. "But getting to the next step—where people grapple with the differences they hear, where not all opinions and experiences are deemed okay and yet no one can lay down the correct answers—is tougher" (83). The staff reached agreement that racist words or behavior—"even unintentional or arguably misinterpreted ones—that affect our students and families are not private voluntary questions but rather central to school talk" (83).

Confronting, or even beginning to work through, the sources and catalysts of racial suspicion and mistrust is grueling and emotionally taxing work. It is also indispensable. Meier sums up the hard work on these issues at Mission Hill School with these words:

> It takes conscious, even unremitting, effort to create communities that resonate equally for people of color. Listening more closely to ourselves and allowing ourselves to be more carefully listened to might go a long way to change the messages that we unintentionally pass on to kids about the color of the world. (90)

OPENNESS

When employees or other stakeholders in a system lose faith and hope, their minds close up like turtles withdrawing into their shells. New leaders, new programs, new ideas are greeted with a single cynical refrain: "This/he/she too shall pass." Or when their hearts are constricted by fear, then caution and suspicion develop into an atmosphere that is poisonous to creativity and collaboration.

But in a climate of trust, the shells begin to open up, and that opening is essential to individual and organizational progress. Where there is openness, there is the possibility that new ideas, alternative approaches, and feedback of all kinds will be considered and perhaps even adopted. Where there is openness, colleagues form deeper and more trusting relationships, allowing for cross-fertilization and the spreading of valuable information and inspiration.

Open, honest communication is simply indispensable to the progress of social systems, such as schools and school districts. It is how they tap into and capitalize upon their collective potential. Trust engenders openness, and openness invites connections, and connections stimulate the innovation that is essential to systemic school reform. And the inverse is true as well: suspicion and fear promote isolation, which prevents collaboration and innovation, thus paralyzing efforts at systemic improvement. When individuals' reservoirs of experience, knowledge, and creative insight are partitioned or iced over, hope hardens and progress crawls and slips.

An opened-up system is alive with change, with the formation of new structures and cultures to support new learning and new applications. Margaret Wheatley expresses it this way:

> The source of life is new information—novelty—ordered into new structures. We need to have information coursing through our systems, disturbing the peace, imbuing everything it touches with the possibility of new life. We need, therefore, to develop new approaches to information—not management but encouragement, not control but genesis. . . . I know of one organization that thinks of information as salmon. If its organizational streams are well-stocked, they believe, information will find its way to where it needs to be. It will swim upstream to where it can spawn. The organization's job is to keep the streams clear, so that the salmon have an easy time of it. The result is a harvest of new ideas and projects. (1999, 96–97 and 100–101)

The challenge is not only to lead in the creation of an open culture, where stakeholders experience the freedom that engenders innovation, but also to *be* open and flexible as a leader and so to walk the talk of openness. Such openness is essential to learning how to lead. Aspiring leaders must observe and reflect on their actions and the consequences that flow from those actions. And, if they are to develop, they must have the flexibility to change their approach going forward if past actions have led to undesired results (Johnson 1996).

This holds true for all leaders in a school system from school board members, union leaders, superintendents, and central office directors and cabinet members to principals and teacher leaders. "I'm far more effective when I get out of my own way," says LaVaun Dennett of Norwalk–La Mirada Unified School District near Los Angeles. "Sometimes when you're trying to control where you're going, you get it all set up, and you don't see other possibilities that are out there, because you've already made up your mind. Being able to stay open is really important, so that you anticipate what might happen and are ready for it when it does."

Positional leaders have crucial roles to play in the formation of open organizational cultures. The adaptive challenges that school system leaders face are too complex to be effectively addressed without leadership and innovation springing up in all levels and areas of the system. Ronald Heifetz points out that "the inclination of organizational systems is to see innovators as threats to the normal way of doing business. That means these deviant voices need a lot of protection because they are at risk of getting clobbered by the organization" (Sparks 2002, 45).

So leaders need to model openness by being visible, open-minded and open-hearted learners, and they need to protect innovators and incipient leaders from the cultural undertow of the status quo. In education in particular, leaders will often need to conscientiously seek out innovative practice if they are ever going to know what needs protecting and to nourish innovation.

The most challenging time in my entire career was my first year as a classroom teacher. Something that helped me begin to make sense of my struggle was an article I read that addressed the extreme professional isolation that is nearly unique to education. Traditionally, and this was very much the case in my experience, the work of teachers has taken place alone with their students, shielded from the view of other professionals other than the occasional supervisory visit from a building administrator. Both triumphs and fiascoes happen in isolation. Because most educational leaders come from the classroom, the culture of isolation has tended to be school-wide and system-wide. The answer to this problem is not to force classroom doors open, but to create an environment where trust is engendered, openness rewarded, and innovation protected and disseminated.

A powerful example of what needs to happen to develop this sort of culture took place in Brazosport Independent School District on the Gulf Coast of Texas. The southern part of this Texas district has much higher concentrations of students in poverty and students of color than does the northern part. In 1991, the disaggregated results of the Texas Assessment of Academic Skills (TAAS) exposed a gaping achievement gap between the northern and southern portions of the district. The district has eighteen schools, and all nine of the schools in the southern part of the district had been designated as "low performing" by the state (Davenport and Anderson 2002, 18).

As district leaders grappled with the stark facts of their newly clarified current reality, they drew upon Effective Schools research and Total Quality Management principles to begin fashioning a strategic initiative to fundamentally change their practice. Among the insights gleaned from TQM was the importance of identifying best practices. They pored over their data and discovered a stunningly successful third-grade teacher. "Despite the fact that 94 percent of her students were considered 'at risk,' virtually all of them had mastered each section of the TAAS" (Davenport and Anderson 2002, 45). This teacher had developed an eight-step, data-driven instructional process that included using assessments to determine what material students had and had not mastered and re-teaching the material until it was mastered (45–49). In Brazosport, this teacher's innovation was not only sought out and protected; it became the basis for school-wide practice that proved successful. It was then used system-wide, enabling the district, over a period years, to close the achievement gaps between students in poverty and their more affluent peers and between students of color and their white peers. According to Patricia Davenport, who was Brazosport's director of curriculum and instruction at the time, some schools in the southern portion of the district are now edging out their northern and more affluent counterparts.

System leaders in Brazosport didn't shelve or try to explain away the bad news that disaggregated student performance data told, but instead responded openly and honestly. And theirs was an open system, in that essential connections were made not only internally but externally as well. TQM didn't come to the district from nowhere; it came as a result of its relationship with the headquarters of Dow Chemical's Texas operations, which provided district leaders with TQM training (Davenport and Anderson, 29). And, of course, district leaders sought out a successful, innovative practice that had been hidden within one of their schools and connected that "best practice" to classrooms throughout the system.

The foundational importance of openness notwithstanding, this is not an argument for unconditional openness. It must always be tempered by discernment and discipline. Openness to anything and everything is a recipe for a state of confusion that can dissipate into anarchy or harden into paralysis. The effective spiritual leader will cultivate an open culture that is leavened by healthy inquiry and a laser-like focus on the core work of continuously improving teaching and learning throughout the system.

SHARED OWNERSHIP

Harvard president Lawrence Summers once observed that "In the history of the world, no one has ever washed a rented car" (quoted in Friedman 2003). But I feel entirely safe in asserting that most people who have *owned* a car for more than a few months have either washed it or paid to have it washed. Ownership affects attitudes and behavior, not only when it comes to possessions but also with respect to participation in a community, organization, or system.

The leaders of the highest-performing schools and school systems, including ones that serve student populations that have generally been underserved in public education, understand the importance of shared ownership. If you've participated in the creation of a vision, a plan, or an initiative, then you are a joint owner, with a stake in its destiny. Then your involvement is not merely a matter of compliance but one of passion and commitment.

For me, this is *the* defining characteristic of an outstanding school: The students and faculty "own" the place, which means that they are committed to its vision and are passionately working to fulfill it. I will never forget my visit, as part of a small group of foundation officials, to Central Park East Secondary School in Harlem. I was impressed with the level of student engagement and the quality of learning we encountered during classroom visits. But what revealed to me the secret of the school's nationally celebrated success was a moment in a group interview with the principal and entire faculty. What the teachers told this group of officials from various foundations, with the principal in their presence, was that if the principal ever tried to pull the school off course, he would be out. The teachers own that school.

Several years before that experience, I was part of small team that was conducting a system analysis of a large urban school district. During our several-day visit, we collected documents, visited schools, and conducted dozens of individual and group interviews with leaders and practitioners at all levels of the system. Even before he arrived, the new superintendent had worked out a comprehensive agenda for district-wide, standards-driven reform. Some teachers had participated on teams that drafted the standards or that reviewed and helped to revise them. But talks with teachers revealed a lack of ownership for the standards and for the overall reform agenda, as well as soaring frustration and sagging morale. How could that be? They had been engaged, hadn't they?

Not really. When the overall agenda is predetermined and rigidly driven forward, real engagement does not occur, even if stakeholders have some influence around the edges of it. Teachers in this district—including teachers who had participated on the standards drafting and reviewing teams—felt that the standards were being imposed on them through a seriously flawed process. No one was listening to their deeper concerns, even though it was teachers who would be on the front lines, either using or ignoring the standards in their daily work (Thompson 1998, 54; Thompson 2003, 242–43).

But what's the alternative? Decisions by a committee of thousands? Fortunately the methodologies for deeply engaging members of a large organization or system in far more effective ways have been developed, tested, and proved successful. The following illustration is a composite account, but that's not to say it is pure fiction. I draw the key elements of this story from the experience of actual school districts and other organizations.

A CASE HISTORY

Janice Kumin became superintendent of the mid-sized, racially and economically diverse Mortondale Unified School District (both Kumin and

Mortondale are fictitious names) on the heels of the previous superintendent's failed reform program.[2] She faced a dilemma. She knew that deep changes were needed to improve student performance across the system, but she didn't want to be run out of town as her predecessor had been. The previous superintendent had been labeled "top-down" and "arrogant." Kumin believed that she could avoid that fate by genuinely engaging stakeholders throughout the system in the development of a vision and set of strategies for carrying it out. Her plan was to collaboratively develop an agenda for improvement based squarely on the results of a community-wide needs and priorities assessment.

Assessing Community Needs and Priorities

With the assistance of outside consultants, an assessment team was organized that represented families and other community members, local businesses and community-based organizations, teachers, administrators, high school students, and central office staffers. The plans to form the team were broadly publicized, and it was put together on a voluntary basis.

The team was trained to conduct focus groups and worked together to develop half a dozen questions that would be used in a series of focus groups, interviews, and phone surveys. Over a period of five months the team spoke with, but mostly listened to, hundreds of Mortondale citizens and employees—including recent graduates and dropouts of the Mortondale high schools—as well as teachers, principals, and currently enrolled students.

In focus groups, participants were asked to identify strengths and needs in Mortondale's schools, discuss changes in society and in workplaces and the implications these changes have for what students need to know and be able to do as a consequence of their school experience, and identify priorities for change. Suspicions and resentments, evident at the outset of these sessions, were often replaced by the end of the two hours with a growing sense of positive investment in the issues relating to the schools.

Reporting Results

What was crucial, once the assessing of needs and priorities was complete, was for the district administration to report on the results to the whole Mortondale community. Working closely with the consultants, the assessment team planned a large-scale event. The event was aimed not only at reporting back but at engaging a critical mass of community members and school system employees in establishing a strategic direction for achieving an agreed-upon mission and set of goals. After more than a month of intensive planning, more than nine hundred individuals—representing employees from every level and corner of the school system as well as parents, business and community leaders, and city officials—came together for two full days. Participants were grouped according to the district's thirty-two schools (with business, city, and central office representatives being randomly and evenly distributed among the school groups).

The team that led the needs and priorities assessment launched the event with a few words of welcome and a brief description of the purpose and goals of the event. Over the course of the two days, the group heard from the school board, reporting on the results of the needs and priorities assessment; the superintendent, who briefly articulated the vision, as she perceived it, coming out of the assessment effort; the teachers' union president, who made some brief observations about the role of teachers in bringing about educational change; and a panel of local business and community leaders, describing the implications that changes in the workplace and family structure have for students to be successful in our rapidly changing world. Each speaker or panel was followed by an opportunity for school groups to process their reactions and identify one or two key questions. These discussion periods were followed by an opportunity for school groups to pose questions to the presenters.

Establishing Strategic Direction

In addition to an overall reporting on the needs and priorities assessment, district leaders presented a draft statement of mission, vision, goals, and strategies, which was drawn from the results of the assessment process (Jacobs 1994, 90). A considerable portion of the first day was devoted to discussions of this statement, in which school groups recorded deletions, additions, and other alterations. In the late afternoon of the first day, these sheets were posted on walls around the meeting space and participants voted—using green and red sticky dots—on which proposals they most strongly agreed or disagreed with.

That evening members of the assessment team and district leaders reviewed the proposed changes, taking particular note of those proposals with the highest number of votes. The statement was revised, retyped, and distributed to the full group early on the second and final day of the large-scale event. Changes in the statement were discussed by members of the assessment team. And then the full group was given an opportunity to offer comments from the floor.

Included in the revised statement were eighteen major strategies. Toward the end of the event, tables were given $2,100 in play money—a $1,000 bill, two $500s, and a $100. The superintendent pointed out that if they tried to pursue eighteen strategies during the upcoming school year (this event took place in late August), they would probably achieve very little. "What are the three or four high-priority strategies for this school year?" Kumin asked. They were to make this determination as a table and vote on them with the play money. Participants placed their bills into whichever of eighteen boxes—each labeled with one of the strategies—their group had selected.[3] The results of that vote determined the district's short-term strategic direction. The people of Mortondale had set the course.

Before the conclusion of the meeting, people had a chance to sign up for one of the following four strategy task forces that would be organized to carry the strategic change initiative forward:

- task force for aligning standards, curriculum, and assessments
- task force for redesigning professional development
- task force for shared accountability
- task force on communications and community engagement

Parents, community members, teachers, principals, and central office administrators were represented on each of the task forces. An important role that these stakeholders played during the sometimes rocky but ultimately successful implementation phase of this effort was to report to, and receive input from, other members of their role group. This helped to keep the channels of communication open and the sense of shared ownership alive.

A significant proportion of the people who made up the Mortondale school system and its community not only voiced perceived educational needs and priorities out of which school system goals were defined, they shaped the agenda for meeting those goals, and many of them—parents, community activists, business people, teachers, and administrators—signed on to roll up their sleeves and do the hard work of implementation. And what the participants learned from living through the ups and downs of implementing whole-system reforms in education prepared them to assume an additional role as spokespersons on behalf of the district's efforts.

Participants in the large-scale event did not climb on boards behind someone else's reform agenda. As co-creators of that agenda, they *owned* it. The momentum generated in mobilizing this system and community is the momentum required to launch and sustain whole-system change in education.

THE INTERRELATIONSHIP BETWEEN TRUST, OPENNESS, AND OWNERSHIP

John Morefield offers valuable cautionary words concerning trust, openness, and ownership: "They are not ends unto themselves." If they don't translate into practices that support the improvement of student learning, such elements as trust, openness, and ownership, in and of themselves, count for very little. Morefield also describes how and why they can be essential to educational progress:

> When trust, openness, and ownership are there, people are willing to take greater risks—personal and professional risks to get better at their practice. They're willing to look honestly at the dark side as well as light side of themselves—areas where they need growth as well as areas where they need to celebrate. Getting better at practice can only happen if you work at it, and you work at it to the degree that you feel valued and trusted and that you have a stake in the work.

Leaders must both inspire trust in others and exercise trust themselves to engender a climate of openness and shared ownership. If leaders demonstrate trustworthiness by walking their talk and leading with integrity, they can successfully nurture trust in the system and community, and out of the soil of that trust grow openness and ownership. But true openness and ownership will not develop if leaders fail to demonstrate trust and faith in their followers and refuse to empower them to open up and take ownership.

Joseph Jaworski distinguishes between commitment that begins with will and a deeper commitment that begins with willingness, surrender, or what Martin Buber calls "grand will" (1996, 133–34). Surrender may sound like a flaccid absence of commitment, and so it is when it refers to a "come what may" attitude of passive acceptance. But Jaworski is talking about something quite different—about a deep commitment to a higher purpose and a humble recognition that the fulfilling of this purpose cannot be humanly controlled. Ownership of, or commitment to, a purpose or vision that cannot be controlled leads to a measure of surrender and involves a high level of trust that the purpose *will* be fulfilled. It also calls for openness or responsiveness to *how* the purpose unfolds, which may veer from our expectations.

Too many educational reform efforts have caved in on themselves. This often happens when new structures are erected on faulty foundations. The groundwork of digging a foundation of trust, openness, ownership, shared vision, and core values is essential if progress is to be sustained. This leads us to the subject of the next chapter: the power of vision and the anchor of core values.

NOTES

1. The article by Cohen (2001) was co-researched and edited by this author, and so the description of Sacramento in this chapter draws on interviews conducted and materials gathered on a site visit to the district by Thompson and Cohen. The article is also available on line: www.aasa.org/publications/strategies/index.htm.

2. This is a variation on a composite that I have used in two previously published articles: "Moving from Publicity to Engagement" (1998) and "Community Engagement: Moving from Words to Action" (2003).

3. The play-money tactic for engaging a large group in setting an organization's strategic direction is one that I observed in a successful large-scale

change event engaging an office of a large federal government agency. The event was designed and executed with assistance from Dannemiller Tyson Associates, consultants on whole-scale organizational change.

REFERENCES

Bryk, A. S., and B. Schneider (2003). "Trust in Schools: A Core Resource for School Reform." *Educational Leadership* 60, no. 6 (March): 40–45.

———. (2002). *Trust in Schools: A Core Resource for Improvement.* New York: Russell Sage Foundation.

Cohen, G. S. (2002). "Sacramento, CA: From Chaos to Achievement." *Strategies* 9, no. 1 (October): 3–7.

Davenport, P., and G. Anderson (2002). *Closing the Achievement Gap: No Excuses.* Houston: American Productivity and Quality Center.

Evans, R. (1996). *The Human Side of School Change: Reform, Resistance, and the Real-Life Problems of Innovation.* San Francisco: Jossey-Bass.

Friedman, T. L. (2003). "Thinking about Iraq. Pt. I." *New York Times*, Jan. 22, A21.

Jacobs, R. W. (1994). *Real Time Strategic Change.* San Francisco: Berrett-Koehler.

Jaworski, J. (1996). *Synchronicity: The Inner Path of Leadership.* San Francisco: Berrett-Koehler.

Johnson, S. M. (1996). *Leading to Change: The Challenge of the New Superintendency.* San Francisco: Jossey-Bass.

Meier, D. (2002). *In Schools We Trust: Creating Communities of Learning in an Era of Testing and Standardization.* Boston, Mass.: Beacon Press.

Payne, C. M. and M. Kaba (2001). "So Much Reform, So Little Change: Building-level Obstacles to Urban School Reform." *Journal of Negro Education* (February).

Richard, A. (2002). "Sacramento Mayor's Legacy: Improved Schools." *Education Week*, February 2.

Sparks, D. (2002). "Bringing the Spirit of Invention to Leadership: Interview with Ronald Heifetz." *Journal of Staff Development* (spring): 44–46.

Thompson, S. (1995). "Needed: New Foundations for New Educational Structures." *New Schools, New Communities* 11, no. 3 (spring): 4–6.

———. (1998). "Moving from Publicity to Engagement." *Educational Leadership* 55, no. 8 (May): 54–57.

———. (2003). "Community Engagement: Moving from Words to Action." *Journal of School Public Relations* 24, no. 4 (fall): 241–53.

Wheatley, M. J. (1999). *Leadership and the New Science: Discovering Order in a Chaotic World.* 2d. ed. San Francisco: Berrett-Koehler.

———. (2001). "Bringing Schools Back to Life: Schools as Living Systems." In *Creating Successful School Systems: Voices from the University, the Field, and the Community*, ed. F. M. Duffy and J. D. Dale. Norwood, Mass.: Christopher-Gordon Publishers.

CHAPTER 6

Groundwork: The Power of Vision and the Anchor of Core Values

Jennie Butchart's Sunken Garden

We stand for a time in her vision,
surrounded by green dark cliffs of cascading ivy
and the lighter green spray of ferns
and wavering threads of falling water.
We wander along dreambeds
where Gooseneck Loosestrife
suspends her spilling snowflakes
and Bearded Tongue displays pink and white coronets,
while the lemon-yellow horns of Angel's Trumpets bow
and Angel's Fishing Rod dangles magenta lures.
Here we see the scarlet-dotted orange orbs
of Scotsman's Purse and the clustered
lavender bells of Grape Hyacinth.

And we cannot completely believe
that this silent eruption
of cultivated magic
began in the gray-clay waste
of a limestone-emptied quarry. (Thompson, 2003)

When my family and I visited the Butchart Gardens on Vancouver Island a few summers ago, we found ourselves under a sort of spell. After a leisurely tour of all the gardens, taking time to soak in their unique beauty, we found ourselves drawn back into them. It was similar to the feeling we've all had when we don't want a captivating novel or movie to end. We were especially entranced by the Sunken Garden. For me it had to do with the experience of standing in someone's vision. I don't mean standing in someone's line of vision, but being in the place where a transforming vision has been fulfilled.

In 1908, when Robert Pim Butchart, a cement industrialist, had emptied a large quarry of its limestone and clay, his wife Jennie went to work in the place—a vast and desolate cubic hole in their property. More than a decade later the waste place had been transformed into the Sunken Garden, which now daily draws and inspires thousands of visitors. This story is not solely about vision. It is also about passion, perseverance, and the interplay of vision and personal mastery. It is said that Jennie Butchart had not been much of a gardener before 1908, but in pursuit of her vision she became a master gardener and the creator of a patch of earth like no other.

The experience in this garden reminded me that the daunting challenges that educational leaders face in the twenty-first century simply cannot be met without the transforming power of vision. The work is to transform obsolete factory-model school districts into systems of schools that accomplish what has never before been accomplished: a high-quality education for all children across the ethnic and socioeconomic spectrum.

Most animals on Earth have the optical ability to visually scan what surrounds them at any given moment so long as they are not in extreme darkness. But according to Jacob Bronowski, our "forward-looking imagination" is what distinguishes humanity from other life forms on Earth (1973, 54). Vision, in this more spiritual sense, is inseparable from the human propensity for exploration, discovery, invention, and creative expression.

The writing and posting of vision statements is a nearly all-pervasive activity in schools, districts, and other organizations required to adapt to changing circumstances. But regardless of the ubiquity of these documents, it appears that comparatively little in the way of genuine visioning takes place in public schools and school districts.

And so we need to make sharp the distinction between a vision statement—words on paper—and the vision itself, which is more of a living power (see Senge 1990, 206). While the vision or mission statement often serves a necessary purpose, the fundamental question—the measure of a vision's power—is what stays in thought or in the heart when you put aside the words on paper. A vision that is original and powerful should plant an image in consciousness that provokes deep feelings, that stirs a sense of possibility and inner commitment.

By inspiring, energizing, and motivating stakeholders, vision serves a vital purpose. Furthermore, as John Kotter has pointed out, a broadly owned, authentic vision unifies diverse participants around a shared aspiration and clarifies direction in the face of shifting agendas and priorities (see Kotter 1996, 68–70).

Where many educational leaders and practitioners have tended to lose course is with the notion that a vision is something that you develop early in a strategic initiative, get on paper, and then only occasionally refer to as you move into the more tangible work of systemic change. There are a number of reasons why this notion widely misses the mark. As we've already indicated, a vision is much more than words on paper. An equally important pair of interconnected points is that genuine visionary leaders understand that meaningful visioning cannot be reduced to a single vision or to an early stage of the change process. Living visions should suffuse and inform every aspect and every phase of educational change. A powerful overarching vision is essential, but it's also important to have visions for the various facets that together make up a system's strategic direction. Visions feed strategic formulation and development, but they are equally essential to every stage of implementation.

FROM INDIVIDUAL TO SHARED VISION

Visions arise in the hearts, imaginations, or souls of individuals. And for some projects—such as a personal garden, painting, or novel—the vision will generally remain with the individual. But if the vision is to drive progress in a social institution such as a school or school system, it needs to be collectively owned. And this raises the question, How does individual vision become shared vision? The answer to this question, of course, is not prescriptive.

A word of warning: The power and collective ownership of a vision will be greatly diminished if the stakeholders' personal visions are given short shrift. Visions for organizational improvement, if they are to be genuinely shared and jointly owned, derive from individual visions (Senge 1990, 211). But the development of personal visions doesn't just happen; they must be actively nurtured and brought forth.

"I think a lot of organizations go through visioning activities, and they assume that individuals have got their own act together," says Les Omotani, who was superintendent of West Des Moines Community Schools when I interviewed him and has since taken on the superintendency in the Hewlett-Woodmere district in New York. He continues:

> When I have had an opportunity to facilitate some of the visioning sessions, I've asked people how many of them over the previous 12 months have spent over an hour actually reflecting and thinking about their own vision of their individual future. You would get virtually no hands up. I would ask them how many spent more than two hours with their travel agent planning a family vacation, and almost every hand went up.
>
> We found that [helping people consider reflective questions] ("What do I really want out of my life? What do I want my legacy to be? Who are the significant people who have shaped and influenced that? Who are my models and mentors? What were their characteristics and values?") opened all kinds of opportunities for them to question, to learn, to think about, to ponder what they wanted to do next as an individual—what was important to them, what their priorities were.
>
> I believe that people who have gone through that kind of experience come to a shared visioning activity from a different orientation than people who haven't. They bring more to the conversations. They bring more passion. They bring more reflection. They bring a greater sense of purpose. They're more certain of what they want the learning community to be like.

Only after personal visions have been broadly cultivated can the work of developing a shared vision commence. And the essence of that work is dialogue. In West Des Moines, Donna Wilkins, the assistant superintendent for teaching and learning, led a team of about eight or ten in the effort to coalesce personal visions into a vision that would elicit the commitment of all. According to Omotani their job was not simply to collect personal visions and fashion a statement that the small team could all sign off on. Rather they would meet with schools and departments, as well as the board of education, and ask key questions:

What is it that you believe wants to happen here? What do you think is important that would be a framework for our learning community? What should our fundamental values be? What's your picture of our culture and our organization if it is to be highly successful?

So we were asking individuals to talk about their own vision of a learning community and what was important to them. Part of it was making sure people were comfortable with each other. This is a very demanding process in terms of building relationships. "What do we want to create here?" We try to capture the images and ideas as people have those conversations.

"What's common?" We also look for what's different and that's part of the diversity. The idea is not to reject something that's different. One of the goals is that everyone can see themselves present in the shared vision. If you reject different opinions too soon the chances are you're not going to end up where you want to be. It ends up being a synthesis of the entire process, but whoever facilitates needs to make sure that they don't reject the diversity too soon.

In the West Des Moines process, the team would gather perspectives from facilitated dialogues, work them into the emerging vision, and send them back to the group for feedback. The evolving vision circulated in and out of the core team, gathering more and more perspectives throughout the process. One challenge in such a process, says Omotani, "is not to get too vested in ownership too early. The goal was not to create a vision that eight or ten people could agree on. It was to create a shared vision that over a thousand people would say, 'you captured it. That is a shared vision I want to make a commitment to.'"

In researching her book *Leading to Change: The Challenge of the New Superintendency,* Susan Moore Johnson explored the experiences and perspectives of twelve new superintendents. One of her findings speaks to the challenge of translating personal vision into a form that encourages broad ownership. As the following summary makes clear, in these instances it was centered to a much greater extent than in West Des Moines around the superintendent, and so we need to reemphasize an earlier point: that the means by which individual visions become shared visions are not prescriptive; there's no one best way.

In translating a personal vision into one that is meaningful in context, the superintendents considered their districts' history and current needs, the character of their communities, the structure and culture of the school organizations, as well as the formal and informal authority inherent in their new position. By defining a vision that was responsive to the local context, each superintendent could better ensure that his or her vision was both fitting and feasible.

From their constituents' perspective, a meaningful vision had to set a direction about something educationally important, it had to be realistic, and it had to have clear implications for action. (1996, 67)

VISION IN ACTION

The visioning process in West Des Moines did lead to three sentences on paper. As Omotani quipped, "we gave in to some words." Here they are:

The West Des Moines Community Schools will be a caring community of learners that knows and lifts every child. We will inspire joy in learning. Our schools will excel at preparing each student for his or her life journey.

Getting the words on paper was by no means the end of visioning for this school system. It was more like a landmark on a never-ending journey. For, as Jim Collins has noted, "there is a big difference between being an organization with a vision statement and becoming a truly visionary organization. The difference lies in creating alignment—alignment to preserve an organization's core values, to reinforce its purpose, and to stimulate continued progress toward its aspirations" (1996).

In West Des Moines the *caring community of learners* piece of the vision is in evidence in community service initiatives. *Knows and lifts every child* is evident in numerous efforts to personalize learning. *Preparing each student for his or her life journey* keeps them attentive to making sure that their educational offerings are actually relevant for all students and broader than academics alone, including community service and exposure to the arts. "Even though we have this high percentage of students who go on to college," Omotani explains, "we're continuing to work very closely with community colleges and businesses for vocational training to make sure that we aren't so biased that we're irrelevant for some kids."

The *joy in learning* element of the vision manifests itself in the system's alternative learning programs, including a summer program called Stretching Minds. This program was initiated for first through third graders in the summer of 2002, with twenty students represented in each grade, and it has been adding another grade each year. It is designed for students who are not experiencing academic success, who tend to come from backgrounds of poverty, and who often exhibit "at-risk" behaviors. The program provides thirty additional days of math and reading instruction over the summer.

"I challenged the staff and the leadership of this program so that if I showed up on any given day and interviewed the children and asked them if they wanted to come back to this Stretching Minds program the next day the answer from anybody I talked to would be 'yes,'" says Omotani. Instruction in this program incorporates project-based, hands-on learning, and students themselves have helped identify activities that they would find enjoyable. At the end of the first year's activities, 90 percent of students and 94 percent of their parents indicated a desire to re-enroll the following summer. In 2003, 96 percent of the students re-enrolled. "Anecdotally," Omotani reports, "there was jealousy from those not accepted. So academically successful students were saying to teachers, 'why wasn't I able to go to Stretching Minds?' Our attendance was incredible. We're trying to make sure that in our pursuit of the highest standards, we don't extinguish the joy of learning."

LEADING FROM CURRENT REALITY TO A POWERFUL VISION FOR THE FUTURE

Success in leading a school district through sustainable systemic improvement hinges on the leaders' ability to mobilize the system in such a way that the distance between current reality and a powerful vision for the future is significantly diminished (Senge 1990, 150–55; Heifetz 1994, 19–27). This strategic work calls not only for building of a shared vision and effectively communicating that vision; it also involves clarifying and communicating the stark facts of current reality. "Most change initiatives that end up going nowhere don't fail because they lack grand visions and noble intentions. They fail because people can't see the reality they face" (Senge et al. 2004, 29).

If the picture of current reality is honest and if the vision is clear and powerful, there should be a significant gap between the two. And that gap between vision and current reality can serve as the source for the creative tension that is required to generate a sense of dissatisfaction with the status quo and the corresponding level of urgency needed to overcome the resistance which change leaders inevitably encounter (Senge 1990, 150).

The process of clarifying and communicating the stark facts of current reality looks a lot like the collaborative effort to develop a shared vision. A large number of diverse stakeholders need to be engaged in this process, so that a variety of lenses are focused on the multitude of facets that together make up the current reality of a system of schools.

THE ANCHOR OF CORE VALUES

Adaptability and flexibility are premium organizational capacities in today's environment of rapidly accelerating change. But where schools and school systems are not firmly anchored, high adaptability and flexibility lead to incoherent flux that can be downright destructive. An organization—any organization—that is unclear about its reason for being and consequently lurches from one fad or program to another is bound to become superfluous or dysfunctional.

Schools and districts, especially in urban areas, are prone to a virtual parade of shifting leaders, and often the appearance of a new superintendent or principal involves contending with a new agenda based on a new vision or set of values. A system of schools that is anchored in a set of core values—an immutable sense of purpose—is uniquely positioned to achieve stability in the face of programmatic and leadership changes.

Educator and noted author Carl Glickman believes that there's a connection between institutional sacredness and institutional sustainability and that while public schools are by definition secular, they can in a certain sense be simultaneously sacred. Glickman says:

Institutions that have a sacredness about their beliefs sustain themselves for a long, long time. People are drawn to such institutions because of faith, because of the belief that this is important. Some of the schools I have studied had that. It was a sacred belief that drew people to it in the same way that a religious institution would draw people. In a religious institution, the sacred core doesn't get broken up because there's a new minister or rabbi that comes in. If they don't work out they go, but they don't take the whole thing down with them.

That's what I'm trying to express in terms of our public schools that have a public purpose. There is a component there of faith that has to do with the belief about the purpose of education and how it is the DNA of a democracy. But relatively few schools see those beliefs explicitly translated into the practices of the school. So there's not an institutional, generational succession around beliefs. Instead, there's a succession around people who may bring one set of beliefs at one time and another set of beliefs at another time.

It's important to make a sharp distinction between goals and values. While goals serve a vitally important purpose, they should be negotiable and, over the long run, they should change. But as Jim Collins has noted, "you cannot 'set' organizational values, you can only discover them" (1996). Values, in other words, do not indicate where we're trying to go; rather, they describe our organizational reason for being.

So while school systems must become operationally agile and structurally flexible, it is essential for that flexibility to be grounded in constancy of purpose. Garmstrom and Wellman point out that "to be adaptive, organizations must continually ask two questions: Who are we? and What is our purpose?" (1995, 6–8). These are the essential questions that define core values, and they can be accompanied by follow-up questions or probes: Are we here for the children or for the paychecks? Do we come to work each day only to tackle discrete tasks or to serve a broader, higher purpose? If the latter, what is that purpose? Is our purpose to help children and young people to become effective test takers and thus to make the schools in our system look good? Or is our reason for being to help children and young people to live meaningful lives and to realize more and more of their intellectual, creative, social, moral, and spiritual potential as members of a democratic society?

Jim Collins suggests using the following questions to distinguish core values from current priorities and preferred practices:

> What core values do you bring to your work — values you hold to be so fundamental that you would hold them regardless of whether or not they are rewarded? How would you describe to your loved ones the core values you stand for in your work and that you hope they stand for in their working lives? If you woke tomorrow morning and had enough money to retire for the rest of your life, would you continue to hold on to these core values? And perhaps most important: can you envision these values being as valid 100 years from now as they are today? . . . If you were to start a new organization tomorrow in a different line of work, what core values would you build into the new organization regardless of its activities? (1996)

What should come out of this process is a shared clarity about what the system and its schools are anchored to. This clarity at the core is freeing, not constraining. "Coherent organizations experience the world with less threat and more freedom," write Wheatley and Kellner-Rogers. "They don't create boundaries to defend and preserve themselves. They don't have to keep others out. Clear at their core, they become less and less concerned about where they stop. Inner clarity gives them expansionary range" (1996, 61).

School systems that gain crystal clarity around their purpose and core values, so that they are recognized and embodied in the work of bus drivers and food service staff as well as teachers, principals, and cabinet members, have been able to maintain a sense of identity and focus across changes in superintendents and school board composition.

This is true in Clovis Unified School District in California, for example, where Floyd Buchanan retired as superintendent in 1991. He translated the district's core values into conversational phrases: "a child's right to an education is not negotiable," "people, not programs," "a fair break for every kid," "educate students in mind, body, and spirit," and "be the best you can be." When a colleague and I visited the district three superintendents and eight years after Buchanan's retirement, the core values were still guiding the district's systemic journey, and we were each given a pen with these same phrases printed on it. The district's long-range goals centered around steadily increasing academic achievement for all students and character development through the Character Counts program.

Since the time of that visit, the superintendent's baton has again changed hands from Walter Buster to Terry Bradley. Bradley's welcome statement on the district website includes the following:

> We in Clovis Unified remain committed to three organizational aims: maximizing student achievement, ensuring a safe and positive learning environment where CHARACTER COUNTS!, and operating with increasing efficiency and effectiveness. Underlying our aims are core beliefs that spur decision-making in our district. We believe that:
>
> - All children can learn and we can teach all children.
> - Everyone is a reader and a teacher of reading.
> - Our values must be more than words.
> - Hard work promotes achievement.
> - It's people, not programs.
> - United as Americans, we value our diversity.
> - We hold ourselves accountable to achieve high standards.
> - Success is an individual journey of continuous improvement.
> - Education is a partnership between the school, the family, and the community.
>
> As one of our core beliefs reads, "Our values must be more than words," and I believe that you will find this demonstrated by everyone in the Clovis Unified School District. . . . We are truly a school district that educates our students in "mind, body and spirit"! (www.clovisusd .k12.ca.us/map/)

During our site visit to Clovis in 1999, associate superintendent Virginia Boris told us that "fractals"[1] provide a window on how the district has achieved and sustained a high level of success and continuity of identity across numerous superintendents. The dictionary definition of a fractal is "any of various extremely irregular curves or shapes for which any suitably chosen part is similar in shape to a given larger or smaller part when magnified or reduced to the same size."[2] A floret of broccoli, for example, is nearly identical in shape to a whole head of broccoli. "The concept of a fractal is that any individual in the organization who really understands the goals and values and their part of the mission can be given a lot of freedom to operate," Boris told us. "You get to a self-organizing concept. As an employee you are given a piece of ownership. You don't have to worry about violating the cultural norms because it's within all of us" (Cohen 1999, 7).

LEADING TO HIGHER GROUND

A couple of years ago I came across well-known words of Winston Churchill, spoken in 1940. They moved me to tears, and I think part of the reason they did is that at some level I had become thirsty for words concerning the nobility of sacrifice in a cultural desert where such words are scarcer than scarce. (When is the last time you heard an American president call upon the whole of his nation to make a sacrifice for something beyond self interest?) Churchill's words:

> Hitler knows he will have to break us on this island or lose the war. If we can stand up to him all Europe may be free and the life of the world may move forward into broad, sunlit uplands. But if we fail, the whole world including the United States, including all we have known and cared for, will sink into the abyss of a new Dark Age, made more sinister, and perhaps more protracted, by the lights of perverted science. Let us therefore brace ourselves for our duties, and so bear ourselves that if the British Empire and its Commonwealth last for a thousand years, men will still say, "This was their finest hour."

That speech was an example of spiritual leadership. It sliced through fear and self-interest to call forth commitment to a higher aspiration and purpose. It cast a moral beam that cut through the fog of war, revealing a pathway for all to "move forward into broad, sunlit uplands."

NOTES

1. For a fuller consideration of the implications of fractals for systemic organizational change, see Wheatley, M. J. (1999). *Leadership and the New Science: Discovering Order in a Chaotic World*. 2d ed. San Francisco: Berrett-Koehler, 123–30.

2. *Merriam-Webster's Collegiate Dictionary*, Eleventh Edition. Springfield, Mass.: Merriam-Webster, Incorporated, 2003.

REFERENCES

Bronowski, J. (1973). *The Ascent of Man*. Boston: Little, Brown and Company.

Cohen, G. S. (1999). *Clovis, CA: Thirty Years and Counting—Sustaining Continuous Improvement* 6, no. 1 (July): 4–7. Also available online: www.aasa.org/publications/strategies/index.htm.

Collins, J. (1996). "Aligning Action and Values." *Leader to Leader*, no. 1 (summer).

Garmstrom, R., and B. Wellman (1995). "Adaptive Schools in a Quantum Universe." *Educational Leadership* 52, no.7 (April): 6–12.

Heifetz, R. (1994). *Leadership without Easy Answers*. Cambridge, Mass.: Harvard University Press.

Johnson, S. M. (1996). *Leading to Change: The Challenge of the New Superintendency*. San Francisco: Jossey-Bass.

Kotter, J. (1996). *Leading Change*. Cambridge, Mass.: Harvard Business School Press.

Senge, M. (1990). *The Fifth Discipline: The Art & Practice of the Learning Organization*. New York: Currency Doubleday.

Senge, M., C. O. Scharmer, J. Jaworski, and B. S. Flowers (2004). *Presence: Human Purpose and the Field of the Future*. Cambridge, Mass.: Society for Organizational Learning.

Thompson, S. (2003). "Jennie Butchart's Sunken Garden." *Reflections* 4, no. 3 (spring): 49–50.

Wheatley, M. J., and M. Kellner-Rogers (1996). *A Simpler Way*. San Francisco: Berrett-Koehler.

CHAPTER 7

Case Study: Transforming a School System

In 1988 when Brian Benzel arrived in Edmonds, near Seattle, Washington, as the new superintendent of public schools, the community was still reeling from what was then the longest teacher strike in state history: thirty days. The strike led to a shake-up of the school board and may have contributed to the retirement of then superintendent Hal Reasby. The explicit point of contention in the strike was overcrowded classrooms, but if you were to scratch deeper, you would find a pervasive feeling among teachers that they were not trusted or respected by district leadership (Thompson 2003).

Two other issues were brewing at that time: (1) Having recently reached the bottom of a nearly 50 percent decrease in enrollment (from 30,000 to around 16,000), the district was expanding again at a rate of about six hundred students a year; (2) the district had been "unable to deliver the full scope of [school] construction projects they promised voters in a recent bond election" (Torrens, 1).

The district now serves close to 22,000 students in 34 schools. More than 26 percent of the students are minorities, about 24 percent qualify for a free or reduced-price lunch, and 13 percent are special education students.

TRUST AS A PREREQUISITE FOR PROGRESS

After the strike was over, superintendent Reasby asked director of student services Stephen Fink to lead a task force of teachers and administrators in delving into the root causes of the strike. Fink agreed to do so on condition that the unvarnished results of the group's quantitative and qualitative research would be openly reported. The task force randomly sampled 10 percent of the teachers' association and wrote up the report. According to Fink, before the time of the strike the district had a top-heavy structure, including a large, centralized curriculum and instruction infrastructure. Teachers felt professionally belittled by the prescriptiveness of what was coming out of central office.

The leaders of the teachers' association were amazed by the candor of the report. In the months following the report, the superintendent retired, along with two of five school board members. And the school board, with two newly elected members, conducted a superintendent search that led to the hiring of Brian Benzel.

Benzel, according to Fink, understood that nothing of lasting substance could be accomplished without the creation of a trusting environment. The honest reporting of the teacher and administrator survey results and the board/superintendent shake-up got the trust-building started, but far more was required to fundamentally alter what had become a culture of suspicion.

REBUILDING CREDIBILITY, TRUST, AND OWNERSHIP

There are a number of actions and processes that were key to the creation of a culture of trust and respect in Edmonds, but what was equally essential was the development of a leadership team that embodied trust by being both trustworthy and trustful. Benzel came to the position with a sense of trust as a core value that he feels was the result of how he was raised by his parents in a small town and in a community of faith. "I relate it to the notion of grace in a Christ-centered sense," says Benzel.

"Brian [Benzel] epitomized a leader with a very strong moral compass and very clear values base," according to Fink, who became one of his assistant superintendents. "One thing about Brian was his presence—he was fully present, every meeting, every step of the way. He led by modeling the trust that was needed."

This modeling of trustworthy leadership is exemplified by Benzel's handling of a threat to his leadership authority that erupted during his first year on the job. A principal, who had some innovative ideas but whose management style provoked fear, gave transfer slips to two of her very capable teachers and accompanied those slips with threats of negative evaluations if they didn't transfer to another school. The teachers reported their principal's action to the teachers' association. When attempts by association officials to intervene got nowhere, they reported the problem to Benzel. He met with the principal and said: "This isn't how we do business. We're not going to do it that way. You need to apologize to these people and not do this any more." In the meeting, she was outwardly compliant.

The next morning, however, Benzel's phone was "ringing off the hook," because the principal had vacated her office and left a note in every teacher's mail box. In the note, the principal claimed that the superintendent had directed her to perform an unprofessional act and that she was leaving. With a notice for insubordination and job abandonment, Benzel fired her. When she came back with doctors' notes claiming that she was in a high state of depression, he worked out an arrangement whereby she would take sick leave for the next year and then retire.

"She never came back, and the teachers' association was flabbergasted that that had happened," says Benzel. "It became a kind of symbolic event where they realized I wasn't going to whitewash or ignore problems in the management team. It's not about trying to ballyhoo a bunch of power; it was just doing the right thing for the institution and our mission."

Susan Torrens, whom Benzel hired as an assistant superintendent and later promoted to deputy superintendent, says in reference to Benzel's handling of the same incident that "it was the consistency of that kind of action that changed the culture."

Principles of Decision Making

As was noted above, the district at the time of the strike had a top-down approach to decision making that tended to make teachers feel marginalized. Early in his tenure, Benzel brought in outside consultants and convened a large group of teachers, union officials, and administrators, as well as food service workers, bus drivers, and custodians, to develop a set of guiding principles for creating a trusting environment. About this effort, Fink says, "We worked from the basis that what is most personal is most universal. Collaboration was never about a process or protocol. It's about a value. It's a value that says that by adding your voice and her voice and his voice and my voice, collectively our voices will be more powerful."

This shared value eventually took form as "Principles of Decision Making," a document that was used at all levels and all corners of the district as a guide for making decisions. The document identifies and elaborates these principles:

- a positive climate
- an inclusive organization
- an effective process
- continuous evaluation

The work around this document, which underwent numerous revisions as it was tested by various parties within the system, was foundational to the institution of distributed leadership and shared decision-making authority in the district. Fink and Thompson summarize:

> Although the district assumed leadership of the effort to create content and performance standards and a multidimensional assessment system aligned with the standards, and although it continues to make key decisions concerning district-wide initiatives, school-level leaders (teachers and principals) are empowered to make budgetary, staffing, and program decisions. Recognizing the uniqueness of each school culture, the district has never prescribed a site-based management policy. Instead, district and teacher association leaders devoted long hours to the formation of a set of guiding principles for ideal decision making, a document that is now in its fifth draft after 10 years of refinement and daily use at all levels of the system. (240)

Trust Agreement

The development and widespread use of the guiding principles for decision making prepared the way for a ground-breaking departure from the typical labor-management contract: a trust agreement. This lean document established "a mutual commitment to creating an atmosphere of trust and respect, nurturing collaboration, encouraging innovation and risk taking with a focus on improvement, providing opportunities for individual growth, and supporting other progressive principles and interests" (Fink and Thompson 2001, 244). The parties upheld their agreement (and continue to uphold it) through continuous bargaining on a monthly basis.

The preamble to the 2001–2004 trust agreement includes this enlightened statement:

> By creating this Agreement we hereby commit to continuing a collaborative relationship which aspires to last beyond the tenure of those currently in leadership positions in our respective organizations. Our Agreement is intentionally general and brief because we believe that the existing relationship is based on sufficient trust and respect that detailed language which can result in lack of flexibility for buildings and staff is unnecessary.

Long before the emergence of the trust agreement as a document, says Benzel, association and district leaders "found ways to find common ground that added to synergy and trust. Instead of talking trust we acted trust." He contrasts this process with a neighboring district that developed a trust agreement between the superintendent and union president that was never broadly owned by their respective followers. "My sense is that you've got to live it and act it before you write it," says Benzel.

Fink says that Benzel "had—and helped me develop—a quite amazing ability to track multiple actions in the present as a way of thinking about the leverage of those actions for creating the future. You are part of the unfolding and so you do anticipate, because much of what you anticipate is relational. It's understanding how people are going to act and react toward this movement we are creating."

Before Benzel was hired as superintendent, Penny Peters, as district negotiator, and Nancy Murphy, as the Uniserve Representative for the Edmonds Education Association, had faced off as adversaries during the strike. Eight years later, they were principal authors of the trust agreement. "That is one of my most delightful quiet pleasures," says Benzel. "We created a set of conditions where the same two people used their same skills in such a powerful and productive way as opposed to a divisive way."

Reviving Community Support

When Benzel arrived in Edmonds, community relations initiatives were in disarray and drastically underfunded. Benzel says that "everyone was basing their story about the district on myth, innuendo, and fabrications." Community expectations around the district's capital requirements, for example, had been shaped by years of declining enrollment. As that trend underwent a complete reversal shortly before Benzel became superintendent, there was not a corresponding communications effort to educate the community.

Under Benzel's leadership, a Citizen Planning Committee was created. It was made up of citizens selected by the PTA or school committee at each of the district's thirty-three schools. The Citizen Planning Committee took on capital planning and the development of program alternatives. District leaders also used focus groups and surveys to clarify their understanding of community concerns and to communicate the district's vision and priorities for action. They hired a strong community relations staff.

System leaders in Edmonds were able to rebuild community trust over time by listening and acting on the information gathered. As a result of the leaders' "modeling a willingness to listen to feedback, revise, and act on feedback given, the community and staff gradually began to believe that the school district leadership valued their input and ideas," notes Susan Torrens, who was Benzel's deputy superintendent before stepping into his shoes when he left in 1997 to take a position elsewhere. "It took several meetings and bond elections before voters put their tax dollars on the line and supported new and remodeled facilities. When they saw the process and the results of the facilities improvements, they continued to support future construction efforts to bring all the district's facilities up to an identified standard" (4).

Along the way, the district discovered that its school calendar is a particularly effective venue for communicating to parents. Under the direction of the newly hired community relations staff, essential information about standards, curriculum, and assessments were woven into the calendar (Fink and Thompson 2001, 245).

Ownership

Torrens, who was hired by Benzel about a year after he arrived, says that her first meeting with administrators was an encounter with people who didn't want to be there: "They didn't want to be thinking about what the vision of the district was. They were not interested in engaging in deep discussion. The underlying purpose of our work was to build the capacities of those people, so that they were engaged, so that they were owning everything that we did."[1]

The district convened business, civic, faith, and community leaders and asked them what they believed students needed to know and be able to do to be successful in life and work. Drawing on the results of the community forums and using an "iterative and inclusive process," the district engaged many teachers and principals in the formulation of a K-12 framework for identifying content and performance standards in all subject areas (Fink and Thompson 2001, 241). The first drafts of these frameworks were intentionally skeletal, but they took on flesh as they passed from school to school and got worked over by teachers and principals, who used the "ideal decision-making guide" to facilitate the process. This standards-setting work took place before most states had even begun to set standards.

As stakeholders throughout the system were engaged in the creation of inclusive processes for making decisions and developing standards, curriculum frameworks, and assessments, they felt increasingly invested and committed to the work. They also felt respected as professionals. There was an increasing sense of joint ownership between district leaders and school-level leaders and staff. Over time the culture was transformed. With the emergence of a culture of trust, shared ownership, and intellectual honesty, openness took root and blossomed as well.

RESULTS

During the nine years that Benzel led the Edmonds School District, a wide array of substantive structural, procedural, and cultural changes were carried out. The literature on educational reform and organizational change indicates that deep reforms tend to provoke resistance, confusion, and even trauma. For this reason it is noteworthy that a 1997 employee survey found that 88 percent of respondents reported that "Edmonds is a good place . . . to work" (Sharp 1998, 82).

The groundwork of building or restoring trust and ownership around a shared vision and core values is not about collaboration for collaboration's sake; it is a foundation for improving the educational performance of students. One significant measure of reform and of leadership for reform is how a system or organization performs *after* a reform leader passes the mantle. Benzel left Edmonds at the conclusion of the 1996–1997 school year, and Torrens, his successor, retired in 1999. The current superintendent, Wayne Robertson, was promoted from within the district, as Torrens had been.

In Benzel's final year (1996–1997) only about 27 percent of fourth graders met math standards according to the Washington Assessment of Student Learning (WASL). But by 2002–2003 the percentage of fourth graders meeting the WASL standard increased to 60. In that same time span, the percentage of fourth graders meeting WASL standards in reading increased from 54 to 72 and in writing from 49 to 56.

The trend for seventh graders was similar. From 1997–1998 through 2002–2003, WASL results for seventh grade climbed from 19 percent to 39 percent in math, from 40 percent to 57 percent in reading, and from 37 percent to 59 percent in writing.

The progress is evident in tenth grade as well. From 1998–1999 through 2002–2003, WASL results for tenth graders rose from 34 percent to 41 percent in math, from 50 percent to 65 percent in reading, and from 44 percent to 62 percent in writing.

The trend for subgroups has, with some exceptions, generally followed the same upward arc. WASL scores in reading for African American fourth graders, for example, climbed from 37 percent in 1997–1998 to nearly 54 percent in 2000–2001. The percentage of African American fourth graders meeting WASL standards in math shot from 7 to more than 24 in the same period. The percentage of Hispanic fourth graders scoring at grade level in math also rose dramatically during the same time frame, from 20 to nearly 36, but Hispanic reading scores in fourth grade, after rising from 46 percent to 54 percent between 1997–1998 and 1999–2000, sank to 44 percent the following year.

REFLECTIONS

Steve Fink's theory of action for systemic school improvement has evolved since his departure from the Edmonds school district, and so, looking back with 20/20 hindsight, he now sees how the district could have done some things differently. The theory of action at the time was that "if we were clear about what we wanted kids to know and be able to do in terms of our standards and if we were clear in terms of our assessments—providing good quality information about kids' perform-ance back to teachers and principals—then we could allow them to find their best path in the spirit of decentralization and shared decision mak-ing. Now I look back on that and say I think that's a flawed theory of action. The district leadership needs to drive and ensure clarity and co-herence along the way."

Fink now believes that with a deeper knowledge of powerful in-structional practice, they could have developed an infrastructure for professional development that could have more rapidly resulted in overall improvement of student achievement and in a more dramatic re-duction in the achievement gap. It's not that he would now move en-tirely away from decentralization. "My point is that it's really about helping teachers in each and every school get smart about what good instruction looks like and helping principals learn to lead that."

Despite his retrospective reflections, Fink strongly believes that the foundational work of restoring a culture of trust, openness, and owner-ship around a clear vision and core values was indispensable. Building on that solid foundation, the system perhaps could have moved more ag-gressively on behalf of students who were not performing well. It's a matter of moral passion and courage in the service of moral purpose—the subject of the chapter that follows.

NOTES

This case study is informed by Fink and Thompson (2001), Torrens (unpub-lished paper), and interviews with Brian Benzel, former superintendent of Ed-monds School District, and Stephen Fink, former assistant superintendent of Edmonds School District, as well as a videotape of a presentation made by Brian Benzel and Susan Torrens (who succeeded Benzel as superintendent) at the June 2000 institute of Panasonic Foundation's Leadership Associates Program. Information was also drawn from the following websites: www.edmonds.wenet.edu and http://reportcard.ospi.k12.wa.us/Reports.

1. Quoted from videotape of a presentation that Torrens made with Brian Benzel at the June 2000 institute of Panasonic Foundation's Leadership Associates Program.

REFERENCES

Fink, S., and S. Thompson (2001). "Standards and Whole System Change." *Teaching and Change* 8, no. 3 (spring): 237–46.

Sharp, L. L. (1998). *Organizational Learning in a K-12 Public Education Setting: 1988–1998.* Ph.D. diss., University of Washington.

Thompson, S. (2003). "A High-Performance School System." In F. M. Duffy, *Courage, Passion, and Vision: A Guide to Leading Systemic School Improvement.* Lanham, Md.: Scarecrow Education.

Torrens, S. (unpublished report). Edmonds School District: A Case Study of Organizational Transformation. Secaucus, N.J.: Panasonic Foundation.

CHAPTER 8

Moral Purpose, Moral Passion, Moral Courage

In 1996, when Larry Leverett became superintendent of Plainfield Public Schools in central New Jersey, it was a low-performing district where twentieth-percentile average performance in language arts and math was considered good enough (Cohen 2001, 13). Under Leverett's leadership most schools in the district adopted America's Choice as a whole school reform model. The organization that created and supports this model, the National Center on Education and the Economy, brought its board of directors to Plainfield in November 2002. At a breakfast meeting with NCEE's board and senior staff, Leverett showed a slide illustrating the steep increase in elementary performance over the previous four years, with the most recent average at more than 77 percent of students achieving state standards. One board member wanted to know what the state average was, and Leverett said, "83 percent."

Another board member then asked how Plainfield fared against demographically comparable districts (the students in Plainfield are 98 percent African American and 70 percent qualify for free or reduced-price lunches). Leverett said that Plainfield was outperforming most other districts in the state with comparable demographics. The board member said, "Because that is the real point of comparison for Plainfield?" Leverett said, "No, sir. Princeton and Millburn are the real points of comparison for Plainfield." The board member said that they set the standard but would not be the benchmark for comparison. Leverett again respectfully disagreed, pointing out that this is about social justice and equity and that the kids in Plainfield need to be prepared to compete with students in Princeton.

The superintendent maintained his poise and a respectful tone throughout this interchange, but there was also a passion about what he was saying that could not be concealed. If I had not spent several hours interviewing Leverett a few days before, I would not have understood the profound depths and dimensions of that passion. His story is about moral purpose, passion, and courage as well as personal transformation and spiritual development.

As an African American, Larry Leverett attended mixed-race public schools in Passaic, New Jersey. Two teachers became towering symbolic figures in his moral landscape: "Martha Camp"[1] and Edward F. Jackson. When he was in ninth grade, Leverett's mother struggled to get him into algebra and Latin and the college track program. "I remember vividly the principal and the guidance counselor who ended up threatening my mother with calling the police and having me classified as emotionally disturbed, but she did not relent from pursuing my placement in those courses. My mother prevailed." He got into algebra and Latin, and his Latin teacher was Martha Camp. During the year that he attended her class, Martha Camp, who was white, never called on Leverett, not even when his was the only hand waving for attention. "Martha Camp became the symbol of what teaching and learning should not be about."

Edward F. Jackson, an African American, was Leverett's fourth grade music teacher. Jackson taught Leverett and his brothers in school and then he began providing group lessons and private lessons to the Leveretts and other students in his home. In high school, Leverett was steered into an armed services rather than a college preparation track. Jackson intervened. He obtained an application for Leverett from his own alma mater, the historically black Virginia State College, brought it to the Leverett house, and helped the family figure out how to prepare for and apply for college. Larry Leverett was the first member of his family on his mother's side and only the second on his father's side to attend college. When at first he was not accepted for admission to Virginia State, Leverett told Jackson, who orchestrated his conditional acceptance and got him a music scholarship to boot.

"Mr. Jackson became the image of what educators should be about," says Leverett. "I've always been guided by what I did not want to be and what I would not tolerate as an educator and by what it looks like if we really want to intervene and help kids and their families to be successful." Leverett's moral passion and sense of purpose around this is palpable. For him moral purpose and social justice are inseparable, and they are the driving force of his work as an educational leader.

Not surprisingly, Leverett's moral development was more complex than the two contrasting archetypes of his own schooling can convey, as potent as they are symbolically. He had been raised in a family and a church that emphasized love and forbearance. He was certainly not raised to be racist.

He attended Virginia State in the 1960s and was swept up in the civil rights movement. He organized students when Stokely Carmichael came to campus. What began to increasingly dominate his heart during these years was not the love that was so strong in his home life, but anger at the injustice of the systems of government and economy that perpetuated inequities. He had, and continues to have, disdain for institutional racism.

These feelings had their roots in his childhood. In addition to negative race-based experiences in school, Leverett remembers family trips on Highway 1 from New Jersey to Georgia with his parents and grandparents. They had to pack enough food for the entire journey, because there was no place for a black family to get a meal along the highway in those days. "I've not only seen the 'colored only' signs," he explains, "but I've witnessed the fear in the eyes of my grandparents that we would violate the 'colored only' rule. We got prepped for our trips south on how to address shopkeepers and on what to do if we had to go into a gas station."

In his second year in college, he switched from a major in music to education. He didn't like what the work and discipline around music study was doing to his sense of pleasure in music. Also, in Malcolm X's words—"Education is the passport to the future, and the future belongs to those who prepare for it today"—he could see the connection between education, social justice, and black power.

After graduating from Virginia State College in 1969 with a degree in elementary education, Leverett went to work as a third grade teacher in the elementary school in Passaic that he had attended as a student. Immediately, he was uncomfortable with how ill prepared he was to help those students who were most in need of help. The school offered no support, and so he took his development into his own hands, enrolling in night classes at Teachers College, Columbia University, and receiving a master's in educational leadership in 1974.

As a school board member in Passaic in 1976, Leverett's approach was confrontational, fed by his anger and hatred of a system of institutional racism that limited opportunities for children and their families based on the color of their skin. But he found his militancy wasn't getting anything done, and so he began a self-reassessment. Several experiences over a period of years contributed to his growth from a racist sense of social justice to a more inclusive and open-minded passion for social justice. One such experience predated his tenure on the Passaic school board. During his academic work at Teachers College, Leverett undertook a research project around his hypothesis that white teachers didn't hold the same expectations for African American and Hispanic students as they did for whites. He made observations of teacher-student interactions at the Urban Crisis Daycare Center in Passaic, but the data he collected did not support his hypothesis.

An even more influential experience in his personal evolution came through his participation in the Passaic Optimists Club, a volunteer service organization. People of Italian, Polish, and African descent, business people, educators, and others worked together to send poor kids to camp. This gave him a tangible experience of working for a shared purpose in a multiethnic group. He now feels blessed to have "met people of all flavors who have strong commitments to social justice, fairness, and equity that are unequivocal, unshakable."

When Leverett's mother was in intensive care for a terminal condition at Passaic General Hospital, he made a commitment to her. He dedicated his career to her, to the woman who saw to it that all five of her children attended college and who "put the value in our hearts about really becoming educated and supported all of us, whatever it required."

Of the dedication of his career to his mother, Leverett says, "I have to honor that—what that means. I have to have integrity in what I do. I have to be moral and ethical. I have to have a really deep sense of commitment and be willing to use all of the gifts that God has blessed me with to do the right thing in education. So, I don't have a job; I just have work. Since I've made that explicit dedication to my mom, I am driven. I think that makes me different."

In the face of injustice and in the passionate intensity of the civil rights movement, the moral foundation, rooted in love and forbearance, that Leverett was raised with was taken over for a time by a sense of outrage whose flames were fed by racial hatred. As Leverett gradually outgrew his fierce rage, his sense of moral purpose and passion were deepened, clarified, elevated. This is the engine of his leadership, the source of the extraordinary energy that his colleagues, close and far, admire.

There is something unique in this story of formally dedicating one's lifework to a person whose sacrifices and gifts can never be repaid. At the same time, in some regards it speaks to moral leadership in terms that are universal—applicable to us all. Moral leadership is rooted in a powerful sense of commitment to a purpose or mission that is too expansive to be confined to self-interests. As Michael Fullan has noted, "to strive to improve the quality of how we live together is a moral purpose of the highest order" (2001, 14).

Moral purpose gives grounding to the efforts and energies that educational leadership demands. It answers the fundamental questions: Why do we, as a school or school system, exist?

MORAL PASSION

In the course of researching this book, I conducted one interview that was an exception to the usual one-on-one conversations. In this instance, I interviewed two educational leaders together, and they each spoke less about themselves than about a man named Richard Green, a superintendent they had worked for in Minneapolis. He later died during his brief tenure as chancellor of New York City Public Schools. Betty Jo Webb, who is now an educational consultant, was a middle school principal in Minneapolis during Green's tenure and knew him socially. JoAnn Heryla, who also is currently self-employed as an educational consultant, worked closely with Green as his coordinator of long-range planning.

Before his appointment as the first African American superintendent of Minneapolis Public Schools, Green was the principal of North High School in the district. Webb describes her earliest impression of him:

> I remember him talking passionately about the city. What I liked about
> him was not so much the content of what he said—although I liked that

too—but I especially liked the depth. His eyes kind of sunk back in his head when he was really passionate about something. . . . What I saw in social settings . . . was that the passion did not change. I remember think-ing that he reminds me of a preacher. He reminds me of a person in the religious sense, especially African Americans, how they get into talking about the Bible, and that's the way he talked about children and educa-tion . . . and the city.

Heryla says, "He was grounded in a belief system and a sense of pur-pose and a vision for making things better for the kids in the school sys-tem."

Webb also describes a dramatic moment at the first school board meeting after Green's promotion to the superintendency: "The evening he was appointed superintendent, he came to the podium. He looked at Ray Arveson [the outgoing superintendent whom the board had just fired]. He did not address his bosses first. He addressed Ray Arveson first, saying 'I want you to know that my day, too, will come.' Then he addressed the board."

At the time of Green's appointment as superintendent, the district was under court order to desegregate its schools. At the same time, de-clining enrollment had contributed to an extremely low fund balance that had adversely affected the district's credit rating. These factors contributed to the formation of a politically charged challenge very early in Green's tenure: the closing of eighteen schools as well as mea-sures to desegregate the schools that remained. What had been happen-ing up to this point, according to Heryla,

> was a constant chess game of moving people around and tinkering and not addressing the issue, not talking about the fact that the district was racially divided. . . . The closing of schools was a moral issue. There was no way that the district could move forward without moving popu-lations of kids around. So the issue of closing eighteen schools repre-sented the understanding of the ethics of the situation and being able to communicate it to the community and taking the closing of schools out of the political arena and moving it into the arena of "this is what's right for the kids in the schools."

I placed this account under the subhead of moral passion, but it is as illustrative of moral courage as it is of moral passion. The two of course are inseparably linked with each other as well as with moral purpose. According to Webb, Green announced the closing of the schools at a huge assembly "in the heart of the city . . . where he honored and respected the [principals] by placing them in a physical position next to him. He survived that with dignity." His passion to do what was best for the children empowered Green to lead courageously.

Moral passion in educational leadership is indispensable because nothing less can answer the urgent need for sustainable progress. Each year of inching, incremental progress in public schools involves educational loss for many children. When a child drops out or disengages or falls hopelessly behind, a blanket of darkness is more often than not thrown over her or his future. And when we consider the vast number of students who are being underserved in our systems of education, it becomes clear that humanity's future is being stunted and constricted.

Allison W. Phinney articulates the urgent need for change in terms that are broader than public education alone, but that speak powerfully to educational leaders:

> Revolutionary change is needed. The ponderous pace of theory and debate is simply too slow to save humanness from being swallowed up in the opportunism of materialism, from being redefined, dispersed, swept away, unremembered. Now we need not so much the historian's late and sober assessment as the poet's, the dramatist's, the human being's passionate outrage and wakened alarm. More primary than each person's self-awareness of national or academic or professional identity—lawyer, economist, educator—must be a readiness to measure one's own consciousness of the human spirit against, not only terrible atrocity, but the equally terrible deadening of morality and spirit that leads to unchecked crimes against humanity and the loss of civilization. (2002, 242)

It is not enough to recognize the importance of closing the doggedly persistent achievement gap in public education. It is not enough to sympathize with the plight of children who are educationally short-shrifted in the name of public education. "Are we touched, or are we moved?" asks Ed Taylor, codirector of the Center for Educational Leadership at the University of Washington. "To be touched is to be a sympathetic observer, to feel pity, to be a kind supporter, to be someone who has learned about and appreciated difference. . . . To be moved is something

else. Being moved requires taking a critical, systemic, and action ori-
ented approach" (2003).

We need moral purpose, a profound commitment to powerfully educate *all* of the children and young people in our care. And that sense of
purpose must ignite and feed the flames of moral outrage and passionate, unflagging leadership to bring justice and opportunity to children
and young people who hold human destiny in their hearts and minds.

And it is not as though we simply need a few morally passionate
souls in our midst, a passionate leader here and a passionate teacher
there. Creating educational systems that powerfully serve the needs and
potentials of all students cannot be done without widespread and sustained commitment fueled by moral passion and rooted in moral purpose. The reason that Betty Jo Webb and JoAnn Heryla are still moved
to tears when they speak about Richard Green is not simply that they
observed his moral passion in action, but that he tapped into and drew
forth their own moral purpose and passion and that of so many colleagues.

"Passion is not an event," writes Derrick Bell, "but an energy; and
it's an energy that exists in all of us, all the time. The question is not
whether we have it but whether we access it, and how we channel it"
(2002, 23–24).

MORAL COURAGE

Derrick Bell was one of only three African American attorneys in the
Civil Rights Division of the U.S. Department of Justice during Eisen-
hower's presidency. During much of the 1960s, he led the NAACP Legal Defense Fund's litigation efforts in the South. From the late 1960s
on, he has been a professor and scholar of law, first at the University of
Southern California. In 1971 he became the first African American to
gain tenure at Harvard Law School. For six years, beginning in 1980,
he was dean of the law school at the University of Oregon. He resigned
from that post in protest when the university refused to grant tenure to
an Asian American woman. At this point he was wooed back to Harvard, but he resigned again in 1990, when the university failed to grant
tenure to any African American women in the law school.

Bell's career is defined not only by his substantial legal and academic accomplishments, but also by the courageous stands he has taken on behalf of social justice. He has laid down his career for his beliefs on more than one occasion. In his autobiography, *Ethical Ambition,* he sums up his career with these words:

> Given the successful ends, it is tempting to assert that I set a clear course with well-defined motives right from the start. Tempting but far from the truth. Many of the decisions that led to what my students see as worthwhile outcomes were not easy to make and seemed as likely to lead to the abyss as to advancement. Going in a direction other than—often in opposition to—the mainstream is often unnerving. I did benefit from the support of a strong family, a wonderful wife, and helpful teachers and role models. No less important was a developing belief that life offers a spiritual foundation of support for difficult decisions, and the actions based on those decisions.
>
> . . . I have worked for success as the world measures success, but my primary goal has been to live an ethical life, or as the hymn puts it, "to live the life I sing about in my song." That means I try to choose the ethical route even when defeat rather than success may wait at the end of the road. In fact, just as I know victory based solely on might is no victory, it is also hard to imagine truly fulfilling success that isn't the result of ethically founded, sustained endeavor. (2002, 5)

The temptations to compromise one's integrity abound in the current educational environment. An unintended consequence of high-stakes, test-driven pressures for improving student outcomes, for example, is the growing temptation to push out—or fail to notice when they are preparing to drop out—those students who are most likely to drag down overall scores or scores within subgroups. Succumbing to this pressure is a sure indicator of moral purposelessness and cowardice. The extent of such practice appears to be considerable. A lawyer for a child advocacy group, for one of many examples, told *New York Times* reporters that she and her colleagues have received cell phone calls from guidance counselors in bathrooms reporting that "they've been told to get rid of kids"—to push them out of school and onto the streets (Lewin and Medina 2003, 1).

The political and social pressure around test scores is intense. It was so when states were the main drivers of accountability, but even more so since the passage of No Child Left Behind. Doing the right thing for children at risk can jeopardize job security, especially if school board members are preoccupied with test scores and the resources that flow or evaporate according to progress as measured by test scores.

"Risk taking is probably the most defining act of an ethical life," Bell points out (50). But it's not enough for school and district leaders to assume political risk by resisting the temptation to push academically unpromising children out of school. The moral purpose of public education can only be fulfilled when children are meaningfully engaged, when their individual promise is recognized and capitalized upon. A significant number of schools and programs have demonstrated that it is possible to reach and engage students who have been at extreme risk of failure. Doing so calls for an all-out moral, political, intellectual, and financial investment in each student. It happens when educational leaders approach the work for each and every child as a sacred trust.

"When I operate from my belief system," says JoAnn Heryla, "that's when I do my best work in creating networks and coalitions or groups to get something done. I also tend to take risks based on what I believe is right. I tend to be far less cautious in that arena than I am otherwise."

Educational leadership is inseparable from moral leadership. "Our work is a moral endeavor," says Stephen Fink, who was assistant superintendent in Edmonds, Washington, before taking on his current work as director of the Center for Educational Leadership at the University of Washington. He continues:

> Our moral purpose is to develop our young people into citizens who can participate in a democracy and chart their own moral course. We can't pick and choose which kids we want to do that with. It must be all-inclusive. You have to have courage around morality. I look back on sixteen years in the Edmonds school district, and I only have one regret: that I wasn't more outspoken where I could have been.

At one time, the leaders in Edmonds had to remove a teacher, who, having gotten drunk, called some female students in the middle of the night and started asking them sexually explicit questions. When the teacher was placed on administrative leave, he hired a lawyer and the district found itself battling on two fronts: (1) the legal battle and (2) the PR nightmare. The district was obligated to protect the man's confidentiality, but he was loved by the community, and parents were enraged, Fink recalls.

They would say, "You're not divulging all that you know." And I would say, "You're absolutely right. And I won't, because as much as I have an obligation to you and your kids, I have a moral and legal obligation to respect the due process rights of this employee. I'm not going to tell you what I know, but I will tell you about what leads us to make the decisions we make. First and foremost is the health and safety of your kids. We will not jeopardize that. We will not compromise that for any reason."

In a certain sense, everyone in a school system from custodian to superintendent and from school secretary to school board president is a teacher. The students and families served are watching and learning — positively or negatively — from the decisions made and actions taken. "We're not just making decisions for ourselves," notes educator and author Timothy Lucas. "We're modeling for the next generation on how we make decisions. That's an unbelievable responsibility."

NOTE

1. "Martha Camp" is a pseudonym

REFERENCES

Bell, D. (2002). *Ethical Ambition: Living a Life of Meaning and Worth.* New York: Bloomsbury.

Cohen, G. S. (2001). "Plainfield, NJ: Moving on Many Fronts." *Strategies* 8, no. 1 (February): 13–16.

Fullan, M. (2001). *Leading in a Culture of Change.* San Francisco: Jossey-Bass.

Lewin, T., and J. Medina. (2003). "To Cut Failure Rate, Schools Shed Students." *New York Times*, July 31.

Phinney, A. W. (2002). "The Dynamic Now — A Poet's Counsel." In *Candles in the Dark: A New Spirit for a Plural World*, ed. B. S. Baudot. Manchester, N.H.: New Hampshire Institute of Politics at Saint Anselm College.

Taylor, E. (2003). "Leadership for Social Justice: Envisioning an End to the Racial Achievement Gap." *New Horizons for Learning* 9, no. 4 (fall). www.newhorizons.org/trans/taylor.htm.

CHAPTER 9

Eye of the Storm, or Clarity in Chaos

And a man shall be as an hiding place from the wind,
and a covert from the tempest;
as rivers of water in a dry place,
as the shadow of a great rock in a weary land.

—Isaiah

System-level leadership in public education is tumultuous work. It is relentlessly intense, enormously complex, and often downright chaotic. It produces storms of various kinds: resistance, controversy, confusion. Slight miscalculations can lead to devastating, unintended consequences.

It's probably not possible to lead a school system from outside the storm. For this reason, it is vitally important to locate the eye of the storm—the still-point in the center, which can be a place of clarity in the swirling crosscurrents and emotional stir of organizational upheaval. "All spiritual traditions teach us ways to find peace of mind and acceptance," Margaret Wheatley notes. "As leaders, we need to find ways to help people work from a place of inner peace, even in the midst of turmoil. Frantic activity and fear only take us deeper into chaos" (2002, 46).

If Larry Feldman's experience is any guide, this "inner peace" or "acceptance" that Wheatley refers to is by no means an indifferent or passive state of mind that says "what will be will be." It does mean that a leader in the eye of a storm can experience serenity in the face of intense pressure and can be a witness to hostilities giving way to unified action.

At the time that I interviewed him, Feldman was a Region Director of School Operations in Dade County, Florida, the fourth largest public school system in the United States. His region included 55,000 students in fifty-one schools. His responsibilities included budget, transportation, attendance, school boundaries, maintenance, capital construction, instruction, training and evaluating school administrators, teacher professional development, referrals, emergency operations, parent problems, grievances, food service, and security monitors.

At a time of intense personal and professional stress, Feldman was saddled with a major school redistricting effort. At that time his own parents were not in good health and his father had to quit work. When Feldman's workday at the school district would end late in the evening, after hours of facing down challenges, he would visit his parents to help them before coming home late to his own wife and daughters. On top of this, he was a doctoral candidate. As he describes it, Feldman would be "working from 6 a.m. till midnight, going home, sleeping, getting up. I was one of those workaholics who doesn't say 'no' but says 'yes, pile it on,' and what suffers is your personal health and everything else."

It was in the midst of trying to manage this already overloaded platter that Feldman was selected to oversee the redrawing of boundaries from four existing high schools to include a fifth high school that was being built in an inner-city, predominantly African American community. The four existing high schools were largely segregated—one being mostly white, another mostly Hispanic, another mostly African American, and the fourth with a largely Haitian bilingual population. Although the proposal did not involve new construction at the elementary and middle school levels, it did mean that elementary and middle school students would be streamed into the new high school according to a new feeder pattern. It would involve busing some students almost fifty miles.

Shortly before conducting a public meeting concerning the redistricting of schools, Feldman attended a weeklong stress reduction program at Kripalu Center for Yoga and Health as part of his doctoral work. He came to the program with a fairly high level of skepticism, but several experiences proved powerful, including a craniosacral therapy session he attended one evening.

During this session the therapist did not touch Feldman, but moved her hands in a massage-like manner several inches away from his body to get a sense of the flow of his energy. Feldman says he left the therapy session both relaxed and energized, and it put him in touch with what he called "a different me—there was a definite awareness of a new serenity—being at peace with myself and surroundings."

The night after his return from Kripalu, Feldman stood in front of a crowd of two thousand hostile parents in Miami Senior High School auditorium. The police were there to intervene if things got out of hand. The superintendent was present, as were the principals of the forty-five schools involved in the redistricting, which excluded a handful of magnet schools. When Feldman began to lay out the agenda for the forum, audience members started booing and yelling epithets. Many of the comments were racially charged.

"I can only assure you that this day now lives in Dade County history," Feldman told me.

As we approached 10 o'clock, people were shaking their heads saying, "This is doable. There is a fair way to do this." I had listened to every single person complain. I had personally taken the microphone and walked to each person. I had listened and rephrased so that everybody understood. . . . It was a different Larry. It was one that was reassuring to them. It was one that understood. It was one that could feel their pain. And yet in some way they felt something coming from me. The same people who at 7 o'clock were yelling and calling me names were the ones telling others to "be quiet. Let him talk. Let's see if we can come up with an idea."

After that [event] I got letters from staff. My own principals were coming by and saying they had never seen anything like that. I don't know what it was. I know that during the entire ordeal I felt very calm, I felt very serene. When things got very hot, I began the breathing exercises [I had learned at Kripalu]. During that next week, I had people—school psychologists, staffing people, consultants for curriculum—saying "Can I just come in and sit in your office while you're working?" I would do my work, and they would just sit there in the chair and come and go as they wanted to. I believe in my heart it had to do with what I learned from Kripalu. Because if I had been my normal self, I would have gotten the crowd antagonized and they would have antagonized me. It would have gotten into a shouting match. That's the normal way you do things when you're fighting hostile groups. I believe that there's something about getting into the inner self. There's something about self-reliance, self-awareness, being content that what you're doing is right.

This is not only a story about a leader who kept his cool in red-hot circumstances. Within three months of that event, all forty-five principals, all forty-five PTA presidents, all forty-five union stewards, and all forty-five school improvement committee chairs agreed to a single plan affecting the communities in all forty-five schools.[1]

Nor is this story unique. Les Adelson had similar experiences when he was a new superintendent of schools in South Pasadena, California, and later during his first year as superintendent of Moreland School District, which is also in California.

A shooting took place during a football game in South Pasadena, and two students were wounded. In a situation not unlike what Feldman had confronted, Adelson was scheduled to meet with seven hundred angry parents and community members in an auditorium shortly after the shooting. Prior to the meeting, emotions swirled, and it seemed that everyone had an opinion on how Adelson should handle the meeting. "People were yelling at me for two days, coming into my office and telling me what I should do," he later told me.

Adelson told his secretary he needed some time alone. He closed his office door and sat at his desk. In his words:

> This is the closest thing I've ever done to meditation. In retrospect, I think I might just call it reflection. And I've even teased that I felt like I had divine intervention. There was something that gave me strength and wisdom. When I sat quietly enough and long enough, it just started coming together. I sat at my computer and wrote a statement, which actually turned out to be a ten-minute speech. The comments I got after the meeting, which went incredibly well, were that it was a defining moment for me as a leader to the community. From that day forward I was treated differently. My board said, "Wow, we didn't know you had that in you." That was a very spiritual experience, really reaching down to the depths.

In his remarks, Adelson acknowledged people's fears and set forth a plan to establish a broadly inclusive task force that would be charged with determining what was needed to move the community forward.

Adelson had a similar experience after becoming the superintendent in Moreland. Shortly after accepting his business manager's resignation, Adelson discovered a $1.5 million budget deficit. A few days later, four hundred angry citizens came to a board meeting to protest the budget crisis. Colleagues later told Adelson that before he walked in "it was chaos. The anger was rampant; the venom was spewing. The tenor of the room was just very adversarial."

Adelson "reached down to the depths" to find his opening remarks, as he had done prior to the meeting in South Pasadena. He pointed out that people didn't really know him, because he'd only been in the district seven months. Then he laid out his core values and convictions. "Keep watching," he told them, "and if I don't do it, you let me know." Of the four hundred people present, only about twenty-five went to the microphone to speak. After the meeting, Adelson received a flood of e-mails saying that he had really changed the tenor of the meeting. He accomplished this by acknowledging the community's concerns, clearly stating his own position on the matter, reassuring his listeners that there would be no mismanagement going forward, and encouraging an ongoing conversation with the public about his progress. "Everyone was expecting a blood bath," remarked one listener. "You just stopped it in its tracks."

There is evidence in Feldman's and Adelson's accounts, as well as from other sources, that experience need not be defined by the vortical intensity of events that sometimes engulf educational leaders. The fundamental questions may be these: *What is going on in my heart? What is my state of mind or consciousness?* And while there is an almost overwhelming temptation, when pressures intensify, to allow external events to define one's state of consciousness, it is possible to resist that temptation. It is possible because experience is far more mental than our senses and rationality would lead us to believe. Evidence pointing to the mental nature of human experience is not entirely anecdotal. As surgeon and Yale professor Bernie Siegel has noted: "Unconditional love is the most powerful stimulant of the immune system" (1986, 181). More recently, neuroscientists have reached similar conclusions concerning the relationship between compassion and immune functions by studying practitioners of Buddhist meditation (Hall 2003).

THE EYE OF HURRICANE BUCHENWALD

Jacques Lusseyran was active in the French Underground prior to being captured by Nazis and imprisoned in Buchenwald.[2] Of the many prisoners that Lusseyran came to know during his time in the camp, one stood out as extraordinarily unique: an old man named Jeremy Regard, who had been a welder. Many years later, Lusseyran wrote about him in an essay that includes the following:

> I see Jeremy walking through our barracks. A space formed itself among us. He stopped somewhere and, all at once, men pressed in tighter, yet still leaving him a little place in their midst. This was a completely instinctive movement which one cannot explain simply by respect. . . .
>
> You must picture that we were more than a thousand men in this barracks, a thousand where four hundred would have been uncomfortable. Imagine that we were all afraid, profoundly and immediately. Do not think of us as individuals, but as a protoplasmic mass. In fact, we were glued to one another. The only movements we made were pushing, clutching, pulling apart, twisting. Now you will better understand the marvel (so as not to say "miracle") of this small distance, this circle of space with which Jeremy remained surrounded.
>
> . . . Each time he appeared, the air became breathable: I got a breath of life smack in the face.
>
> . . . It was necessary for there to be a man as simple, as clear, who had gone to the depths of reality, in order to see the fire and beyond the fire. . .
>
> When Jeremy came to us across Block 57, in the midst of his little halo of space, it was clarity which he gave to us. It was an overflowing of vision, a new vision. And that is why we all made way for him. . . .
>
> One went to Jeremy as toward a spring. One didn't ask oneself why. One didn't think about it. In this ocean of rage and suffering there was this island: a man who didn't shout, who asked no one for help, who was sufficient unto himself. (Lusseyran 1999, 146, 148, 149, 150)

Let us pray that no one ever again confronts a storm of hatred, brutality, and fear as overwhelmingly intense as the Nazi death machine.

My reason for including a portion of this account is this: It demonstrates that even in the most extreme hurricane of human horror there was still an eye. It was possible even in Buchenwald for an individual to hold onto a state of consciousness that was defined by something other than external forces.

Lusseyran gives us a few glimpses of how this was done: "Jeremy taught me, with his eyes, that Buchenwald was in each one of us, baked and rebaked, tended incessantly, nurtured in a horrible way. And that consequently we could vanquish it, if we desired to with enough force" (151).

The objective events that surround one are quite often beyond one's control, especially in a complex social system such as a school district. But the subjective experience of these forces and events within consciousness is something that can be controlled. Another passage from Lusseyran illustrates: "The Nazis had given us a terrible microscope: the camp. This was not a reason to stop living. Jeremy was an example: he found joy in the midst of Block 57. He found it during moments of the day where we found only fear. And he found it in such great abundance that when he was present we felt it rise in us. Inexplicable sensation, incredible even, there where we were: joy was going to fill us" (152).

According to his account, Lusseyran too found the eye of the hurricane called Buchenwald: "I perceived, one day like the others, a little place where I did not shiver, where I had no shame, where the death-dealers were only phantoms, where life no longer depended on the presence of the camp or on its absence. I owed it to Jeremy" (154).

When Jeremy moved into a jam-packed barracks with a halo of space around him, he became the eye of the hurricane, a source of peace for the desperate prisoners who surrounded him. Apparently others learned from him how to find that eye within themselves, to locate "a little place . . . where life no longer depended on the presence of the camp or on its absence." Skilled spiritual leaders not only find the eye within themselves, they help others to find a place of clarity in the face of chaos.

THE SPIRITUAL SELF VS. "ME, INC."

It may be that this "little place" that Lusseyran located was in fact a different self, a deeper self. Larry Feldman said that when he stood before the hostile crowd in the packed high school auditorium, "it was a different Larry" and he also spoke about "getting into the inner self."

The shallow self—the ego self—focuses on protecting and defending "little old me" from crushing storm forces and from the sting of insults. Metapsychiatrist Polly Berrien Berends calls it "Me, Incorporated" or "Me, Limited." According to Berends, "Judgment by appearance sires Me, Inc. in every one of us" (1983, 8).

Religious traditions the world over point to a deeper self, which is actually more selfless, because it focuses not on "Me, Inc." but on the bigger picture, whether that bigger picture is defined as the common good, social justice, a larger purpose, the wholeness of creation, or the Creator and His/Her universal family. As Berends has noted, "Life forces us to look deeper for the fundamental reality from which we derive our uniqueness and which alone can harmoniously govern us in relation to each other" (11).

When we do free ourselves, to an extent, from Me, Inc., we not only perceive and experience more of the wider world of possibilities—the truth the ego blinds us to—but we also discover something more of who we are as spiritual beings. "I think most of us have to struggle with the fact that the ego is there," says John Morefield. "I understand that the ego is only one part of myself. I do have a spiritual reality, a spiritual self, that I know is more than just ego."

In my own experience, I've had the clearest glimpses and strongest experiences of spiritual being when, through spiritual study and prayer, I've been able to resist the gravitational pull of the worldly world and so to come into a different consciousness. For me it's been a matter of reawakening to the awe-inspiring magnitude of the Creator's creation. Then the baggage of the ego-self falls away and a less encumbered spiritual self starts coming into focus.

Noted cognitive psychologist Eleanor Rosch of the University of California at Berkeley describes a way of reconnecting with the inner self, or what she terms "original being":

> If you follow your nature far enough, if you integrate and integrate, if you follow your nature as it moves, if you follow so far that you really let go, then you find that you're actually the original being, the original way of being. The original way of being knows things and acts, does

things in its own way. When you get even a glimpse of it, you realize that we don't actually act as fragmented selves the way we think we do. Nothing you do can produce this realization, can produce the original way of being. It's a matter of turning to it and it's a way of acting. It actually has a great intention to be itself (so to speak), and it will do so if you just let it. (Rosch, n.d.)

NEW SELF AS THE FRUIT OF STRUGGLE

For some people in some circumstances, the letting go that brings one to the inner self or "original being" may come from inner struggle as much as peaceful reflection. The Biblical story of Jacob and Esau provides an example that has spoken to millions of students in the various Jewish and Christian communities across the centuries.

Esau and Jacob were twins, but as Esau was the firstborn, he stood to inherit the bulk of his father's wealth. But when Isaac, the now-blind father of the twins, was preparing to bless his elder son, Jacob deceived him and received the blessing of the firstborn that was intended for Esau. Furious, Esau vowed to kill his younger brother. At his mother's urging, Jacob fled to live with his uncle Laban in a distant region. Eventually, Esau came after Jacob, who sent an apologetic message. But the response to that message showed that Esau was coming with four hundred men, intent on revenge.

That night Jacob sent his young family and his possessions across a gorge. What followed could be described as his dark night of the soul. In the words of the book of Genesis:

> So Jacob was left alone, and a man wrestled with him there till daybreak. When the man saw that he could not throw Jacob, he struck him in the hollow of his thigh, so that Jacob's hip was dislocated as they wrestled. The man said, "Let me go, for day is breaking," but Jacob replied, "I will not let you go unless you bless me." He said to Jacob, "What is your name?" and he answered, "Jacob." The man said, "Your name will no longer be Jacob, but Israel, because you strove with God and with men, and prevailed." (Gen. 32:24–28)

As Jacob was alone, it is clear that he was not literally wrestling with another human being. Given the seriousness of his betrayal of his father and brother, and the fact that his own young family was now at mortal risk, it seems reasonable to conclude that he was wrestling with his conscience—confronting the ego-self that had gotten him into this fix. But what may have begun as a wrestling match with his conscience apparently developed into a struggle with the "better angel of his nature," to adapt a quotation from Abraham Lincoln. As Marchette Chute summarizes, "He fought; and he proposed to keep on fighting until he had wrested a blessing out of his travail" (1969, 69).

The blessing that comes from this night of struggle is a new self. The New Oxford Annotated Bible points out that "in antiquity it was believed that selfhood was expressed in the name given a person. Jacob's new name signified a new self: no longer was he the Supplanter but *Israel,* which probably means 'God rules'" (Metzger and Murphy 1977, 43).

The end of the story? At daybreak, Jacob saw Esau coming with his four hundred armed men. But the violence that this approaching storm threatened to unleash dissipated. As Esau approached, Jacob bowed himself to the ground seven times. "Esau ran to meet him and embraced him; he threw his arm around him and kissed him, and they wept" (Gen. 33:4).

My point in recalling this story is to emphasize that reaching one's spiritual self at the eye of the storm may require considerable self-examination and struggle. According to Parker Palmer, spiritual progress requires "honest self-scrutiny first, and then confession, an offering up of our own inner darkness to the source of forgiveness and transformation" (1983, 2). This is the inner work of leadership, and it has the capacity to open possibilities that would otherwise be wholly concealed by the raucous surface of the storm.

What came through in my interviews with Feldman, Adelson, Morefield, and others was that when they looked deeper they discovered that the hostilities they confronted were not about Me, Inc. And what I think is so significant for educational leaders is not only that they could come through these storms without psychological scars, but that the storms dissolved so that, in some cases, hundreds of people came into a place of increased clarity and meaning. That is spiritual leadership. It comes from a deeper place: spiritual selfhood, original being.

CRISIS INTERVENTION: "THE BEST JOB IN THE WORLD"

Cheri Lovre received a telephone call from a staff member of Columbine High School during the deadly rampage that shook the nation. She counseled the staff member for about twenty minutes and faxed a chapter from her book on catastrophic events. Then she climbed onto a plane and went to work with devastated families and staff members in Littleton, Colorado.

On September 11, 2001, it was about 6:00 a.m. where Lovre lives in Salem, Oregon, when the Twin Towers were struck. She had been asleep when a colleague called and said, "I think you should get in to work now." Several days later she was in Lower Manhattan and northeast New Jersey, leading teachers, students, and administrators to a place where they could begin to come to terms with a new reality.

Lovre goes to schools that are reeling from tragedies, such as spates of suicides, and works with people who are lost in unspeakable depths of pain and bereavement. This is her full-time work, and so you will understand my astonishment when she said the following to me:

> It is the loss issues for people that make my job the best job in the world, because when I go in, even the highest administrators are humbled. And suddenly a lot of the turf issues and divisions are out the window, while everybody really does stop. I have the best job in the world, because I get to bring the deepest part of myself spiritually into the secular world at a time when people thirst for it. . . . I have this privilege that every time I walk into a school, I get to breathe spirit into that life, that moment, that encounter. I get to take that with me wherever I go, whether that's what's on the table or not.

In the early 1970s, Lovre began doing art and play therapy with school children with behavioral disorders. In one school, in 1974, the principal suddenly wanted to add another child to the group. When she asked why this was being suggested on such short notice, Lovre learned that the child had witnessed his father's murder at the hands of the child's uncle over the weekend. She arranged to work with this child individually. Soon thereafter, she found herself doing grief counseling for groups of school children.

In 1978 she was awarded a Child in Crisis grant and could work with any child dealing with any death issue: loss of parent, anticipated loss of parent, or the child's own terminal illness.

Sometimes there was a lot of overlap, because — if you start with a group of kids whose parents are terminally ill — as those parents die, those kids don't want to leave their friends and go to a new group. So the groups transition in an interesting way. It was like leaves falling off trees into a moving river. And the leaves would just flow around each other and every once in a while some would separate off. Streams of children moved through my life.

That was the point at which I went through my own personal, emotional, psychological, and absolutely spiritual transformation. Because I began then standing by the bedsides of dying children, kids on my caseload who were dying, and going to funerals; sometimes too many. And I realized that I have a child at home who didn't make me go into anything sad, and I needed to be able to go home and throw my arms open and say, "Hi, honey, I'm here," and not, "Oh, sweetie, I had a tough day."

When a child on my caseload died, I was probably working with siblings as well. So I got to this point at three or four months of having probably 40 or 45 or 50 kids in my caseload where internally I felt like I had a whole army of wind-up monkeys marching in my chest and that I would just explode if I stopped being stressed. If I totally relaxed, I would explode.

She had written three hours a week of consulting time into her grant. This was time for her own sustenance, nurturing, and therapy, and she used this time to work with a spiritual coach.

The transformation was at times heart-shatteringly painful. There were moments when I felt like my body was there, and there was nothing left. At that time I was already doing yoga and meditation, and I started doing some walking meditation and slowly started grounding my meditation into my everyday being. If I was walking across the room in a play therapy group, I could walk across that room with my connection to my Source.

In my conversations with Lovre, she spoke often of the Source. When I asked her what this meant to her, she explained as follows:

The Source is this living, breathing thing. The Source is in every breath. The Source breathes life into us initially . . . the breath of life. The Source is like this unending flow that you can be in or not, and you get to choose. It's never not there for anyone. And we can tap into it in so many different ways. It's greater than I can define and greater than I can know. It is divine. It entirely transcends and imbues our human experience. We can walk in our knowing of the divine. The Source is remarkably abundant.

The spiritual coach that Lovre had begun working with told her, "You need to find something you can do every day to prepare yourself for the day."

For me that meant preparing myself for extremely difficult pieces in terms of kids, but it also meant doing it in a way that allowed me to stay entirely connected to what would sustain me. I started sitting every morning when I woke up, and I came to two meditations that I still do today.

Shortly after 9/11, Lovre was working in a district in Bergen County, N.J., where many parents commute daily into lower Manhattan, and where several community members had been lost when the towers came down. She worked with a group of students, talking through their questions, and then she did a two-hour session with staff members. "People were coming out of their shock and into the reality," she later told me.

At the end of every other session we would sing. This time, they were sobbing so hard that, at first, they couldn't sing. We made it through the song, and as always happens, people came forward and had questions they didn't want to ask in front of the group. These five women came down and stood, and all of them had tears running down their face. I looked at them and raised my eyebrows. And nobody said anything, and I said, "Is there just a single thing that I could help you put into words?" One woman said, "This is the first moment I've felt hope, and I just wanted to stand with you."

Some months later, Lovre wrote out some reflections on her experiences in the aftermath of 9/11. They included the following:

It is as though we each came to earth to play one part of the great symphony. And we each studied the music and learned our instruments before we came. And we touch down here on earth and move along, thinking we know the song. And we do. And then something horrific happens, and it rocks us to our core. Shakes us to our foundations. And while we're waiting for the dust to settle, we can't remember where we were in the playing of the symphony. And we're not sure of our part. And then the Source sends us someone who knows the whole score. And then we're reminded of the Whole, and It invites us to re-remember our own part. And we can do this because we are only a part. And my Sacred Contract is to be so very open to these people who come into my path that I can fully trust that I'll know enough of the Whole and be able to sense enough of their parts that I can bring them the inspiration to go back to sit with the orchestra and once again take up their own instruments so the playing of the song of life will go on.

SPIRITUAL ANCHORING

After Larry Feldman stood in peace for three hours before a hostile crowd of two thousand in a high school auditorium, staff members came to sit in his office. At the conclusion of a post-9/11 workshop, five women wanted to stand with Cheri Lovre. There is reason to believe that people working in our schools and central offices are hungry for peace and clarity. They seek a peace that is not simply the absence of conflict, but a peace that is a presence, a clarifying spiritual presence.

It takes the inner strength that results from spiritual practice to stay open-hearted and steadily focused on a higher purpose when assaulted by opponents or engulfed in a crisis or inundated with trivial necessities. Developing a spiritual approach to educational leadership is not likely to eliminate all stress or prevent political storms or avert crises. But it can provide invaluable anchoring for withstanding storms and staying focused on the high goal of improving education for all students

NOTES

1. Unfortunately, a politically motivated school board member who was up for re-election opposed the plan as it would change his constituency, according to Feldman. "A whole fight occurred. It all fell apart, and the board voted

to leave it alone and define the boundaries somewhere else." While this end-note says something sad about school board politics, it seems to me that the power of what was accomplished before the board got involved speaks for it-self.

2. Lusseyran was completely and permanently blinded at age eight. Re-markably, when not yet out of his teens, Lusseyran organized and led a student resistance movement during the Nazi occupation of France.

REFERENCES

Berends, P. B. (1983). *Whole Child/Whole Parent.* New York: Harper & Row.

Chute, M. (1969). *The Search for God.* Harrington Park, N.J.: Robert H. Sommer Publisher.

Hall, S. S. (2003). "Is Buddhism Good for Your Health?" *New York Times Magazine,* September 14, 46–49.

Lusseyran, J. (1999). *Against the Pollution of the I: Selected Writings of Jacques Lusseyran.* New York: Parabola Books.

Metzger, B. M., and R. E. Murphy, eds. (1977) *The New Oxford Annotated Bible.* New York: Oxford University Press.

Palmer, P. J. (1983). *To Know As We Are Known: Education As a Spiritual Journey.* San Francisco: HarperSanFrancisco.

Rosch, E. (n.d.). *Primary Knowing: When Perception Happens from the Whole Field; Interview with Professor Eleanor Rosch.* www.dialogonleadership.org/interviewRosch.html.

Siegel, B. S. (1986). *Love, Medicine, and Miracles.* New York: Harper & Row.

Wheatley, M. J. (2002). "Spirituality in Turbulent Times." *The School Administrator* 59, no. 8 (September), 42–46.

CHAPTER 10

"What Power Had I Before
I Learned to Yield?"

A Milkweed

Anonymous as cherubs
Over the Crib of God,
White seeds are floating
Out of my burst pod.
What power had I
Before I learned to yield?
Shatter me great wind:
I shall possess the field.
                    —Richard Wilbur

Is it possible to control a complex organization, such as a public school system? I join many other observers and practitioners in concluding that the notion of being in control of any social system is either an illusion or else it is so heavy-handed as to stifle the innovation, openness, trust, ownership, and energy that are essential to organizational health and progress.

Does a leader's experience of coming to terms with the illusive nature of control necessarily have to be disempowering? Or is there power to be found in moving beyond the illusion of control? If so, what sort of power is that, and what is a leader's role in relation to this power that is beyond our control?

The word *power* is loaded with associations, and many of these have to do with political opportunism, manipulation, hierarchical dominance, and even psychological intimidation. The word has also come to be associated with the amassing of wealth via greed and corruption more than through creativity and hard work. *Rich* and *powerful* are the closest of siblings in contemporary parlance. Phrases like *power hungry, power base, power plays,* and *power politics* do not connect naturally in our minds with images of *collaboration* and *distributed leadership.*

At root, of course, the word is quite free from negative associations. The Old French *pooir* traces back to the late Latin *potere,* which means "to be able." The connotations of *power* and *powerful* alter significantly when we move away from organizational settings to art, culture, and nature. To say that a novel, a painting, or a film is powerful is to say that it has a considerable impact on the heart and mind—that it doesn't leave us where it found us.

Or try this: close your eyes and see what comes to mind after reading this phrase: "the sun came out today after days of overcast weather." It would be difficult to overstate the power and importance of the sun to humanity. Not only does the life of our planet depend upon its vitalizing and sustaining daily influence, it also feeds our hearts and souls, allowing us to live our days in light and color. Solar power cannot be grabbed and hoarded, and who would want to, when it must patiently be collected from an inexhaustible source?

What if our sense of power in our professional lives in human organizations was not about competition for a scarce resource, but distribution from a limitless source? "Because power is energy, it needs to flow through organizations; it cannot be bounded or designated to certain functions or levels," writes Margaret Wheatley. "What gives power its charge, positive or negative, is the nature of the relationship. When power is shared in such workplace designs as participative management and self-managed teams, positive creative power abounds" (1999, 40). But when power is hoarded, manipulated, or selectively allocated on political grounds, creative energy is sucked out of the organization, and what fills the vacuum is politics as usual.

"Power isn't a piece of pie. The more power you give away, the more you have," says former principal John Morefield. "There isn't really a lot of institutional or positional power left in the principalship." The same goes for superintendents and their cabinet members and for union leaders and school board members. "But there is tremendous opportunity for referent power and moral authority—that kind of power that comes with building community."

DISTRIBUTING LEADERSHIP, IGNITING INNOVATION

In chapter 5, we explored the interrelationship between trust, openness, and ownership. We said that together these conditions are an indispensable foundation for systemic progress in education. Without mutual trust and respect between leaders and followers, distributed leadership is not possible. And shared ownership is not possible if leaders tightly hold power and decision-making authority. In this way leaders may elicit their followers' compliance, but not the level of commitment that opens the way for innovation and deep change. Edward Wragg expresses this point with a colorful illustration: "Compliance is essentially a conservative notion, because it reflects past practice and rules out novelty, other than that permitted by the authorities, who cannot possibly have a monopoly of the best ideas; in medicine, compliance would have simply ensured the permanent survival of the leech as a form of treatment" (quoted in Rasch 2002, 2).

The distribution of leadership authority is a way of marrying power to freedom. In such an environment, the leadership power or authority of a superintendent or principal is not diminished but enhanced. Instead of being a leader of followers, she or he is a leader of leaders.

Balancing Autonomy with Accountability

Wedged between San Diego and the Mexican border lies the largest elementary school district in California: Chula Vista, serving twenty-four thousand students in kindergarten through sixth grade. Nearly half of these children qualify for a free or reduced-price lunch, and about a third are learning English as a second language. When Libia Gil arrived as the new superintendent in 1993, she found that the district was underserving a significant number of students, but she also discovered that the community generally did not share her sense of urgency. She felt that things needed shaking up, "a sense of disequilibrium" (Cohen 2001, 8).[1]

Gil brought in an outside consultant to help engage internal and external stakeholders in a fresh examination of the system's needs and
priorities. They conducted eighteen focus groups with students, parents, teachers, principals, senior citizens, school board members, business and community leaders, and others. These conversations were the
basis for drawing up a shared vision, values, and strategic goals for
the system. And the process served as a wake-up call to the community:
that change was needed and that change was coming.

The strategic goals included the following: "Collaboration: With the
school as the center, the entire community will become full partners in
education, responsible for each child's success." Gil says that the
school system she inherited had operated in a fairly traditional, top-
down manner, but the "school as center" idea represented a clean break
from the old way of doing business. Assistant superintendent Dennis
Doyle compared the challenge of moving in this direction to "disas-
sembling the old industrial model—the one best way—and trying to
create a new model from the ground up" (Cohen 2001, 9).

The new model involved the fusion of system-level, standards-based
accountability with school-level autonomy in defining school philosophy, instructional practice, governance, and decision-making
processes. Gil, Doyle, and their colleagues discovered that promoting
school-level autonomy had significant system-level implications. In
time, the central office was redesigned and streamlined, so that the administrative budget now comprises less that 5 percent of the total annual budget as human and financial resources increasingly shifted to
schools. More importantly, central office roles and responsibilities
changed from an emphasis on monitoring and compliance to service
and support.

While all schools were held accountable for results, using multiple
assessments aligned with state standards, schools were free to adopt or
design whatever school reform models or instructional techniques they
believed would work best for the particular students they served. The
district includes thirty-nine schools. Of these, four adopted the accelerated schools model; three, the "Comer" model (School Development
Program); two, the microsociety model; and another, direct instruc-
tion/corrective reading. One school created a unique standards-based
model, and five worked with the Ball Foundation to fashion a new

model around the foundation's principles of productivity. Five other schools became district-sponsored charters, which meant that they remained within the district's accountability system but enjoyed an even higher level of autonomy with respect to state and district policies and services.

What about the bottom line—student performance? Using multiple measures to assess student performance, the district has seen steady progress in language arts and math since the 1997–1998 school year. That year only 44 percent of students were meeting standards in Language Arts and Math. The number has increased each year since: 49 percent in 1998–1999; nearly 52 percent in 1999–2000; over 56 percent in 2000–2001; over 57 percent in 2001–2002.

District leaders recognize that they are still far from reaching their goal of a school system where all students meet standards, but steady progress in the right direction counts for a lot, given the trials and tribulations of school reform efforts over the past several decades.

Unleashing Innovation

In some school districts, charter schools are viewed as the enemy. In Chula Vista they are part of the diversity of schools that have sprouted in the creative space that resulted from the dispersion of leadership authority. An even more striking innovation occurred in Calaveras County, California, where district leaders empowered another perceived enemy of public education—namely, home schoolers.

As in almost any public school district, a small proportion of taxpaying parents had pulled their children out of the Calaveras County public schools and were educating them at home. In the early 1990s, Ron Lewis, the associate superintendent, reached out to two of these parents, Linda Mariani and Nancy McKone, and asked them to research the needs and desires of local home schoolers (Gersen 2003). Both of these women were certified teachers who had educated their own and others' children at home. They spoke with dozens of families who had chosen the home school route and then organized their findings in a report to the school district.

This report became the basis for the creation of a new K-12 school, called Mountain Oaks School, which is part of the district but serves families who previously home schooled their children. Mountain Oaks School, which serves 379 students (about a third of whom qualify for a free or reduced-price lunch), "has no classrooms, no formally scheduled classes, no formal discipline code, no classroom teachers, and no report cards," according to Wayne Gersen. "Instead of these traditional trappings of 'school,' it provides home schooling parents with a network of services, and home-schooled students with a network of learning opportunities" (30).

Mountain Oaks School is primarily located in two small warehouses, which include offices, a computer lab, a library, a "conference/seminar/ classroom/ kitchen room," an art studio, a lounge for secondary students, and "storage space for consumable learning materials that students and parents can access when they wish, using an honor system" (30). Gersen explains why overcrowding is not an issue at Mountain Oaks, despite the small physical plant:

> Instead of scheduling classes that meet regularly, Mountain Oaks schedules ad hoc workshops that meet as needed and where needed. The topics of the workshops range from formal instruction in foreign languages and preparation seminars for California's high school exit examinations to introductory units in crafts and interdisciplinary lessons in poetry, geography, and art. The workshops are often held off campus in private homes, in nearby public parks, or in community centers. They are offered for parents and students, in some cases together and in other cases separately. Most of the workshops are offered to multi-age groups of students, recognizing that twelve- and eighteen-year-olds can learn introductory pottery skills or foreign languages together, and that children of all ages can sing or play instruments together. The workshops not only teach academic content, but also provide students with an opportunity to develop social skills and meet with peers. (30)

While the school doesn't have classroom teachers, as traditionally defined, it has "a faculty of mentor-teachers, each of whom is assigned up to twenty-five students. A mentor-teacher . . . serves as a combination case manager, counselor, and guide for a student and his or her parent. . . . At the beginning of each semester, the mentor-teacher helps the parent and student develop a personalized learning plan that defines the learning standards the student will master in the coming weeks and the means of measuring progress toward the standard" (30).

I haven't had an opportunity to visit or study this school. But based on Gersen's description of it, there's a strong possibility that I would enroll my own daughter if we lived in proximity to it. Mountain Oaks avoids a chief downside of home schooling—social isolation and privatization—and, at the same time, it has broken free from the encrusted routines of factory-model schooling that make student engagement so difficult.

The school district had no control over home schoolers, and this hybrid school is not something the district controls. But by empowering parents to give shape to something new, the district has brought hundreds of home-schooling families back into the public system and provided the resources for the creation of a unique learning environment.

"While we worry about designs and structures, tweak procedures and rules, insist on compliance and control, we never succeed in creating an organization by these activities," write Wheatley and Kellner-Rogers in *A Simpler Way*. "Organization wants to happen. Human organizations emerge from processes that can be comprehended but never controlled. . . . Organizations spiral into form, cohering into visibility. . . . This is where we need to gaze, into the origins that give rise to such diversity of form" (1996, 77, 87).

REALISTIC EMPOWERMENT

An organization that goes too far in the direction of empowering all employees to be autonomous decision makers ceases to be an organization. It either dissipates into chaos or becomes a bunch of loosely associated independent, rather than interdependent, actors. An organization that is led through unadulterated command-and-control mechanisms, on the other extreme, stifles its own creative potential by undermining employee commitment and inhibiting risk taking. But an organization that remains coherent and interdependent, while at the some time genuinely empowering its people, has extraordinary potential for high performance.

Educational leaders who understand the critical potential *and* the limitations of empowerment will neither oversell nor underplay this essential dimension of organizational change and improvement (Argyris 1998). There is a balance that must be achieved rhetorically as well as demonstratively.

Superintendent Les Omotani describes what this looks like in West Des Moines Community Schools:

> You can't predict what might happen tomorrow or what the right choices and decisions might be. The illusion of control is just that. That's not to say that a learning community shouldn't have rules and structure to help it be effective and efficient. Our goal is to be a culture of commitment rather than a culture of compliance. We believe that the more that we have to rely on anything that is in the compliance mode, it's probably an indication that we didn't do a very good job of supporting the kind of learning that should be going on.
>
> . . . We have all the typical policy books and handbooks and rules and regulations. We've got all of those classic pieces. What we try to do is to see how many of those can we make go away. We talk on a regular basis about which ones are no longer appropriate, because they don't describe the way we want things to be. The guiding principles are an excellent example. We want to be guided by principles rather than rules and regulations. We'd rather move toward shared vision than be directed by a five-year strategic plan. When people are motivated to close that gap between current reality and a shared vision, everybody gets to lead.

Chris Argyris compares much that happens in the name of empowerment to the emperor's new clothes: "We praise it loudly in public and ask ourselves privately why we can't see it" (1998, 99). He warns about the "inner contradictions" that inevitably sprout where leaders seek to develop inner commitment by empowering employees. "If the inner contradictions are brought to the surface and addressed, they can be dealt with successfully; that is, they will not inhibit the kind of personal commitment that management says it wants. But if contradictions remain buried and unacknowledged, as they usually do, they become a destructive force" (101).

Argyris offers valuable guidance for those who would realistically increase the commitment of employees through the distribution of power:

- Don't undertake blatantly contradictory programs. For instance, stop creating change programs that are intended to expand internal commitment but are designed in ways that produce external commitment (or mere compliance).
- Understand that empowerment has its limits. Know how much can be created and what can be accomplished. . . . Be clear about who has the right to change things. Specify the likely limits of permissible change.
- Realize that external and internal commitment can coexist in organizations but that how they do so is crucial to the ultimate success or failure of empowerment in the organization. For instance, external commitment is all it takes for performance in most routine jobs. Unnecessary attempts to increase empowerment only end up creating downward spirals of cynicism, disillusionment, and inefficiencies.
- Calculate factors such as morale, satisfaction, and even commitment into your human relations policies, but do not make them the ultimate criteria. They are penultimate. The ultimate goal is performance. [In education, of course, high performance is inseparable from pervasive, high-quality student learning.] (105)

Empowerment, distributed leadership, devolution of decision-making authority—whichever term of art you choose—is a perilous path if pursued cavalierly. But a genuine commitment to and thoughtful pursuit of this way of working is quite simply indispensable to developing the depth and breadth of commitment that whole-system educational improvement calls for.

NOTE

1. The article by Cohen (2001) was co-researched and edited by the author of this book, and so the description of Chula Vista in this chapter draws on interviews conducted and materials gathered on a site visit to the district by Thompson and Cohen. The article is also available online at www.aasa .org/publications/strategies/index.htm.

REFERENCES

Argyris, C. (1998). "Empowerment: The Emperor's New Clothes. *Harvard Business Review* (May–June): 98–105.

Cohen, G. (2001). "Chula Vista, CA: A System of Student-Centered Schools." *Strategies* 8, no. 2 (November): 8–11.

Gersen, W. (2003). "The Networked School." *Education Week,* December 3, 30–31.

Rasch, K. (2002). "Beyond Compliance: Creative Inspiration from Overseas." *AACTE BRIEFS* 23, no. 17 (December 16).

Wheatley, M. J. (1999). *Leadership and the New Science: Discovering Order in a Chaotic World.* 2d ed. San Francisco: Berrett-Koehler.

Wheatley, M. J. and M. Kellner-Rogers (1996). *A Simpler Way.* San Francisco: Berrett-Koehler.

CHAPTER 11

Humility in High Places

Humility like darkness reveals the heavenly lights.

—Henry D. Thoreau

Great spiritual leaders in traditions throughout the world are distinguished by, among other things, their humility. When Moses was called to lead his people out of captivity, he responded, according to Hebrew scripture, with these words: "Who am I, that I should go unto Pharaoh, and that I should bring forth the children of Israel out of Egypt? . . . Oh my Lord, I am not eloquent, neither heretofore, nor since thou hast spoken unto thy servant: but I am slow of speech and of a slow tongue." And when Jeremiah was called to prophesy, he protested with these words: "Ah, Lord God! behold, I cannot speak: for I am a child."

What of Jesus, who according to Christian tradition, was anointed "above thy fellows" as Christ? "I can of mine own self do nothing," he is recorded as saying, and "Why do you call me good? No one is good but God alone."

The importance of humility is by no means unique to Western spirituality. As Lao Tsu observes in the Tao Te Ching:

Know honor,
Yet keep humility.
Be the valley of the universe!
. . . The sage is shy and humble—to the world he seems confusing.
Men look to him and listen.
He behaves like a little child.

There's a simple explanation for the universality of the indispensability of humility to powerful spiritual practice. A self-absorbed or self-promoting overinflated human ego is not so adept at yielding to and recognizing powers and possibilities that are far greater than itself. Also, take a careful look at your ego when it has gotten puffed up—it happens to us all from time to time. What you will find at those times is an ego filled with illusions. Its windows on what is spiritually possible are clouded by self-delusions. Humility clears the windows and opens a door into a deeper experience of reality.

But a question remains: Is this talk of humility feasible, or even relevant, to the sophisticated demands and complicated sociopolitical context faced by those who would lead complex organizations in the twenty-first century? It is, and I base this conclusion on research, not just personal conviction.

Jim Collins and a research team of twenty graduate students spent many thousands of hours over a five-year period researching the best-selling business book, *Good to Great*. Out of 1,435 companies, they found just eleven that met the good-to-great standard. After a period of performance somewhere in the good to mediocre range, these eleven companies broke through to greatness, meaning they achieved market returns that at least tripled returns of the general market for fifteen straight years (Collins 2002, 2–7). Most of those thousands of hours of research and deliberation that Collins and his research associates devoted to this effort were spent trying to determine what distinguished these organizations from their peers. This work included identifying eleven comparison companies in the same industries that never rose to greatness.

Several counterintuitive essentials of good-to-great organizations emerged, including so-called Level 5 leadership. All eleven good-to-great companies had Level 5 leaders, but none of the eleven comparison companies did. Level 5 leaders combine personal humility with a "ferocious resolve, an almost stoic determination to do whatever needs to be done to make the company great" (Collins 2002, 30). According to Collins and his research team, personal humility and professional will are two sides of the same coin. The Level 5 leader is powerfully focused on—and relentlessly committed to—something larger than self. It makes sense that there would be a precise, proportional relationship between selflessness and devotion to a larger purpose.

Consider also the words of civil rights lawyer and legal scholar Derrick Bell, who on numerous occasions has been willing to place his commitment to social justice above job security: "Humility gives us space to see that we do not have all the answers, even in our so-called areas of expertise; it lets us listen and respond to what is actually happening, being said, being felt" (2002, 164–65).

The relationship between all of this and leadership was eloquently expressed by Army Chief of Staff Eric K. Shinseki on the day of his retirement, June 11, 2003. During thirty-eight years as a soldier, Shinseki was awarded two Purple Hearts and rose to become the highest ranking Asian American in United States military history. His final observations as Army Chief of Staff included the following: "You must love those you lead before you can be an effective leader. You can certainly command without that sense of commitment, but you cannot lead without it. And without leadership, command is a hollow experience, a vacuum often filled with mistrust and arrogance" (Quoted in Shanker 2003, A32). The general is telling us that leadership is impossible without the love and humility that enable the leader to be committed to his or her followers. If Shinseki is correct about the relationship between arrogance and mistrust, it becomes clear how critical some measure of humility is to the successful leader, given the paralyzing influence that a lack of trust breeds, as detailed in chapter 5.

MEEKNESS REVISITED

It is sometimes said that educational leadership is not for the meek. I would suggest that that statement should be turned on its head. The problem is that meekness has too often come to be associated with weakness and faintheartedness. And it is certainly true that educational leadership in the twenty-first century is not for the weak and faint of heart. But the sort of meekness that spiritual masters have embodied over the centuries is not about weakness, but an inner strength that enables one to remain outwardly calm in the face of attack or retribution. I would argue that it is tremendously relevant to the work of leading an organization through the complexities of change.

Consider Collins's description of a Level 5 president of the United States and a Level 5 CEO. He doesn't call them meek, but captures well what I mean by the word. Collins notes a certain duality in Level 5 leaders. They are at once modest and strong, humble and fearless:

> To quickly grasp this concept, think of United States President Abraham Lincoln (one of the few Level 5 presidents in United States history), who never let his ego get in the way of his primary ambition for the larger cause of an enduring great nation. . . .
>
> While it might be a bit of a stretch to compare the good-to-great CEOs to Abraham Lincoln, they did display the same duality. Consider the case of Colman Mockler, CEO of Gillette from 1975 to 1991. During Mockler's tenure, Gillette faced three attacks that threatened to destroy the company's opportunity for greatness. Two attacks came as hostile takeover bids from Revlon, led by Ronald Perelman, a cigar-chomping raider with a reputation for breaking apart companies to pay down junk bonds and finance more hostile raids. . . . Had Gillette been flipped to Perelman at the price he offered, shareowners would have reaped an instantaneous 44 percent gain on their stock. Looking at a $2.3 billion short-term stock profit across 116 million shares, most executives would have capitulated, pocketing millions from flipping their own stock and cashing in on generous golden parachutes.
>
> Colman Mockler did not capitulate, choosing instead to fight for the future greatness of Gillette, even though he himself would have pocketed a substantial sum on his own shares. A quiet and reserved man, always courteous, Mockler had the reputation of a gracious, almost patrician gentleman. Yet those who mistook Mockler's reserved nature for weakness found themselves beaten in the end. In the proxy fight, senior Gillette executives reached out to thousands of individual investors—person by person, phone call by phone call—and won the battle. (22–23)

Leaders engaged in transforming school systems are continuously surrounded by pressures, resistance, and conflicting forces. They have been and will be attacked, and sometimes these attacks will take on a personal tone. The leader who reacts viscerally will multiply the trouble he or she is trying to mitigate. This is one reason why meekness matters.

Ronald Heifetz and Marty Linsky conclude their book *Leadership on the Line* with a chapter entitled "Sacred Heart." It's about the importance of preserving innocence, curiosity, and compassion in the face of the tumult and dangers that leaders encounter daily. It includes a personal experience that Heifetz had that opens up the significance of what I am referring to as meekness.

Heifetz had been invited to give a speech on leadership in Oxford, England. After delivering the speech, he traveled with his wife Sousan through the English countryside. This took place during Rosh Hashanah, and it was their intent to attend synagogue services once they reached London. Along the way, however, they found themselves enchanted by the village of Castle Combe. Here, as sundown and the onset of Rosh Hashanah approached, they discovered an old Anglican church that they entered. Ron sat in the front, "a Jew in an Anglican church, facing Jesus on the cross" (2002, 228). They had recently attended a Jewish workshop on "deep ecumenism," during which they learned that "sacred heart" is an expression of "God's promise, not to keep you out of the fire and the water, but to be with you in the fire and water" (228).

> Ron looked up at the man being tortured for his beliefs — a frightening sight perhaps for anyone who has not been acclimatized to it, but more so for a Jew, conscious of a history of persecution. After decades of feeling a smoldering outrage with the violent abuses of Christianity, Ron found sitting in that church a very challenging leap across a deep divide. As he reflected on his complex feelings, he began to wonder what this holiday might have been like for Jesus in his lifetime. He thought a bit wistfully, "You were one of our teachers. Why not keep each other company on the New Year? Nobody else is here to celebrate with us."
>
> Ron stared at Jesus and meditated. "Reb Jesus," Ron mused, "Will you tell me your experience on the cross? This is Rosh Hashanah, when we contemplate Abraham's willingness to sacrifice his son, Isaac. Will you please give me a message?" [Reb is an endearing form of the word rabbi, which means teacher.] (299)

Heifetz continued his meditation for about ten minutes and then excitedly asked his wife to come outside with him. They lay side-by-side on the grass, looking up at the blue sky through the branches of a large pine tree, their arms stretched out spread-eagle fashion.

After a few moments, he turned to her.

"How do you feel?" he asked.

"Really vulnerable," she said.

"Me, too. And that's it! That's the message. That's what we learned about sacred heart—the willingness to feel everything, everything, to hold it all without letting go of your work. To feel, as Reb Jesus felt, the gravest doubt, forsaken and betrayed near his moment of death. To cry out like King David in the wilderness, just when you desperately want to believe that you're doing the right thing, that your sacrifice means something, 'My God, my God, why have you forsaken me?' But in nearly the same instant, to feel compassion, 'Forgive them, Father, for they know not what they do.' Jesus remained open."

A sacred heart means you may feel tortured and betrayed, powerless and hopeless, and yet stay open. It's the capacity to encompass the entire range of your human experience without hardening or closing yourself. It means that even in the midst of disappointment and defeat, you remain connected to people and to the sources of your most profound purposes. . . . A sacred heart is an antidote to one of the most common and destructive "solutions" to the challenges of modern life: numbing oneself. Leading with an open heart helps you stay alive in your soul. It enables you to feel faithful to whatever is true, including doubt, without fleeing, acting out, or reaching for a quick fix. Moreover, the power of a sacred heart helps you to mobilize others to do the same—to face challenges that demand courage, and to endure the pains of change without deceiving themselves or running away. (229–30)

It takes the inner strength that I am calling meekness to stay open-hearted and steadily focused on a higher purpose when assaulted by opponents or inundated with trivial necessities. Meekness in this sense is closely tied to personal humility and a steady devotion to a higher calling.

Before we leave the crucifixion of Jesus, there is another lesson to consider—a lesson that transcends sectarian or theological divisions, a lesson that could be as relevant to an atheist as to a devout Christian. Had a newspaper reporter been present at the crucifixion of Jesus, what would the headline have been? Perhaps "Radical Rabbi Killed; Followers Disperse," or simply, "Movement Comes to Brutal End." A couple of thousand years later, it's plain to see how extremely mistaken the second headline would have been.

At the moment of death and dispersion, extraordinary imagination or faith would have been required to foresee that the movement was far from over—that it would have a shaping influence on the contours of tens of centuries and into the future as far as humanity now can see. This illustration brings to mind one of the most famous headlines in American history: "Dewey Defeats Truman."[1]

The lesson is about keeping the long view in focus when current events are pounding home a particular message. As Arnold Toynbee observed, "The things that make good headlines attract our attention because they are on the surface of the stream of life, and they distract our attention from the slower, impalpable, imponderable movements that work below the surface and penetrate to the depths. But of course, it is really these deeper, slower movements that, in the end, make history, and it is they that stand out huge in retrospect, when the sensational passing events have dwindled, in perspective, to their true proportions."

What feels inevitable sometimes isn't. What looks hopeless can sometimes become the threshold of transformative progress. Meekness and spiritual maturity provide the kind of lens that enables leaders to see past the bleak headlines to a more accurate accounting of what can be and perhaps what will be.

CAN HUMILITY AND MEEKNESS BE DEVELOPED?

The question of relevance resurfaces but from a different angle. Is our position fixed on a psychological scale from genuine humility/meekness to extreme egotism/arrogance? Or, are humility and meekness attributes that can be developed, regardless of our conditioning in another direction?

Collins believes that some people have the potential to develop into Level 5 leaders and others do not:

My hypothesis is that there are two categories of people: those who do not have the seed of Level 5 and those who do. The first category consists of people who could never in a million years bring themselves to subjugate their egoistic needs to the greater ambition of building something larger and more lasting than themselves. For these people, work will always be first and foremost about what they get—fame, fortune, adulation, power, whatever—not what they build, create, and contribute.

The second category of people—and I suspect the larger group—consists of those who have the potential to evolve to Level 5; the capability resides within them, perhaps buried or ignored, but there nonetheless. And under the right circumstances—self-reflection, conscious personal development, a mentor, a great teacher, loving parents, a significant life experience, a Level 5 boss, or any number of other factors—they begin to develop. (36–37)

Educational consultant and former principal John Morefield, on the other hand, says that he has always assumed that "humility, like empathy, can be learned."

One of the most powerful and hopeful trends in educational thinking and research in recent decades has been the thoroughgoing challenge to the old orthodox notion that intelligence is genetically fixed. There is increasing evidence that intelligence can be developed. That is not to say that intelligence gets developed simply because it's possible to do so. It requires persistent effort and the building of confidence that results from that effort. And it is deeply influenced by expectations—the students' own expectations, and the expectations of their parents and teachers.

Perhaps, in the same way, humility and meekness can be developed—either by all, as Morefield implies, or by some, as Collins posits. I have come to believe that one way to increase humility and meekness is through spiritual experiences that enlarge one's sense of the powers and possibilities that extend beyond what a preoccupied human ego is able to perceive. It calls for discipline. This discipline might be applied to spiritual study, reflection, prayer, meditation, or whatever enlarges one's perception of the boundless magnitude of the Creator's actual creation.

Parker Palmer describes leadership as an inner journey. He says that "the great gift we receive on the inner journey is the certain knowledge that ours is not the only act in town."

Not only are there other acts in town, but some of them, from time to time, are even better than ours! On this inner journey we learn that we do not have to carry the whole load, that we can be empowered by sharing the load with others, and that sometimes we are even free to lay our part of the load down. On the inner journey we learn that co-creation leaves us free to do only what we are called and able to do, and to trust the rest to others' hands. With that learning, we become leaders who cast less shadow and more light. (1990)

As indicated previously (in chapter 1), spiritual leadership involves perceiving deeper levels of purpose, meaning, and experience than can be materialistically perceived. In other words, without spiritual listening, seeing, and sensing, there can be no spiritual leadership (Kahane 2001, 25). And without some measure of humility, there can be no spiritual listening, seeing, and sensing. Although Collins doesn't suggest this, and I have no research basis for asserting it, my hunch is that this truth may be a root explanation for why all eleven of the good-to-great companies that Collins identified were led by individuals distinguished by their humility. It may be that they were able to listen, see, and sense at a level that was wholly inaccessible to their more egotistical counterparts at the comparison companies.

In humility we may come to a stunning realization: that how reality is fundamentally set up and how things actually happen in that reality are dramatically different from what the arrogance of the human ego would allow us to perceive.

A WORD OF CAUTION

Beware the self-appointed or self-proclaiming humble spiritual servant. Where there is genuine humility, there is a recognition that no matter how much one is learning in terms of leadership, spirituality, or whatever, it must be used with care, because there is so much still to learn, and there is real respect for the dignity of others. Where there is false humility, there is danger, as Carl Glickman notes:

> I have seen in my career people who are regarded as the embodiment of pure selflessness and spirituality. They were put on a pedestal and were not questioned the way you would question other people, because they were seen as people who were so good and so pure. Whenever anyone puts anyone else up on a pedestal, there's danger behind that. There's a lot of cruddy stuff that happens at times when a person is regarded as

having a source of spirit that is so admirable that we don't ask further questions. I have seen people use that to violate other people in very, very terrible ways.

Glickman adds that "if humility makes one open and vulnerable to other people, then it's pure." Then there are no pedestals, or, if there is one in the making, the leader refuses to get onto it. He or she tears it down.

NOTE

1. The conventional wisdom in the final days of President Harry S. Truman's campaign for reelection to the White House was that he would be defeated by his Republican challenger, Thomas Dewey. A famous picture shows the triumphant Truman holding a newspaper with the mistaken headline in bold print: "Dewey Defeats Truman."

REFERENCES

Bell, D. (2002). *Ethical Ambition: Living a Life of Meaning and Worth.* New York: Bloomsbury.

Collins, J. (2001). *Good to Great: Why Some Companies Make the Leap . . . and Others Don't.* New York: Harper Business.

Heifetz, R., and M. Linsky. (2002). *Leadership on the Line: Staying Alive through the Dangers of Leading.* Cambridge, Mass.: Harvard Business School Press.

Kahane, A. (2001). "How to Change the World: Lessons for Entrepreneurs from Activists." *Reflections* 2, no. 3 (spring): 16–29.

Palmer, P. J. (1990). "Leading from Within." www.teacherformation.org/html/rr/leading.cfm?dsp_mode=print.

Shanker, T. (2003). "Retiring Army Chief of Staff Warns against Arrogance." *New York Times*, June 12, A32.

CHAPTER 12

A Vision: Educational Rain Forests

I conclude with my own vision for education. A vision, as we said in chapter 6, is not words on paper. I think you will agree that the three paragraphs that follow do not belong on a plaque or stapled to a strategic plan. What follows could be re-crafted into a vision *statement,* but the precise words of any vision will always be secondary to what the vision itself—the picture of a possible future—evokes in the hearts and souls of a community.

On a recent hike through the Hoh Rain Forest, on Washington's Olympic Peninsula, I was fascinated to see that some of the towering and rotund trees in the forest were maples. If the typical neighborhood maple that now stands by the garage where I live had taken root and grown to maturity in the richly nourishing context of the rain forest, it would now be something remarkable—larger than life. I can get one arm all the way around the maple by the garage. But if that tree had grown up in the rain forest, I wouldn't be able to reach my left hand with my right around the trunk. The maple in my yard is certainly taller than the garage beside it, but in the rain forest, if I leaned back, I would scarcely be able to see the top of the botanical skyscraper. There, every inch of the surrounding forest would be spilling over with life.

If we go far enough—farther, perhaps, than ever before—in the creation of cultures of trust, openness, and shared ownership that are deeply rooted in visions and core values, we will achieve a kind of educational rain forest, with profusions of innovation and knowledge creation; a superabundance of learning; spontaneous, new connections between seemingly disparate fields of study; streams of inspiration, feeling, and realization; hidden springs of motivation; and continually proliferating leadership that is spiritually and morally passionate, courageous, and visionary. In this educational ecosystem, all of our children will thrive in vast expanses of possibility and their minds will reach into heights of creative insight beyond what we can now imagine.

I believe—heart and soul—that a possible human future includes such educational rain forests. I also believe that there's no getting there from here without getting real about spiritual leadership, which uncovers the wholeness that is hidden within reach.

Index

About the Author

Scott Thompson began his career as a high school English teacher in St. Louis County, Missouri. He is assistant director of the Panasonic Foundation, a corporate philanthropy devoted to the transformation of public education in the United States; editor of *Strategies*, an issues series by the Panasonic Foundation in cooperation with the American Association of School Administrators (http://www.aasa.org/publications/strategies/index.htm); and president and a founding trustee of the Glen Rock Public Education Foundation. Prior to joining the Panasonic staff, he was director of dissemination and project development with the Institute for Responsive Education and editor of *New Schools, New Communities*. His previous writings on education and leadership have appeared in *Phi Delta Kappan, Educational Leadership, Education Week, Educational Horizons, New Horizons for Learning, Teaching and Change, Teacher's College Record, The Community Education Journal, The Christian Science Monitor, The Journal of School Public Relations, Education Digest*, various books, and elsewhere.